TEN

Transforming Life Series
Capturing The Heart Of Your Wife

John DePasquale

Contents

Acknowledgments

My grandfather on my mother's side was a fine cabinet-maker in Europe before he moved to this country. I can remember a large cabinet he made that was given to me. It ended up in our basement deteriorating for almost twenty years. One winter, I decided to restore it — almost redeem it, in a sense — from its shabby condition. I literally took it apart and worked on every part. It took a lot of work and patience on my part, but the finished product now looks so much better.

In many ways, the process of writing this book was similar to the restoration of this beautiful cabinet.

Flora Kueppers, a family friend was like the coarse sandpaper I used on the cabinet. She took my often-illegible writing with run-on sentences and made it readable. I owe her many thanks for volunteering to do this.

My older son's wife, Somerlie, was like the fine sandpaper I used to finish the cabinet and get it ready for staining. Her gentle touch and artistic creativity made the words flow, giving them more life and meaning. I am extremely grateful for her insight and enthusiasm.

The cabinet was like my family for a number of years. They were in the basement of my life, I'm sad to say. When God entered my life, He helped me to move my family into first place.

I want to acknowledge my wife Rita, who has demonstrated the reality of Scripture to me in her life. I want to thank her for her total commitment to our marriage, her forgiveness of my broken past, and her continuous prompting for me to become the man God intended. She is the reason I have a story to tell.

I also want to acknowledge my sons, Jared, Adam and Peter, Adam's wife Carrie and Peter's wife Rachel. Their love and acceptance has made being a father one of the greatest joys in my life. Thank you all for being men that I can be proud of. I am so proud of the way you show your love for your families and for each other. You do it so well.

I would also like to acknowledge my friend, Gregg Dedrick, who has prompted and encouraged me to write during our many years of friendship.

Lastly and most importantly, I thank God. He is certainly the God of second chances. The Holy Spirit never grows weary in helping me become more like Jesus. I can sum it all up from the book by Charles Dickens, *A Christmas Carol*. In the last scene when Scrouge is with his nephew and his nephew's new wife, he quietly whispers, "God forgive me for the time I have wasted." For in which I can reply for me, "He has forgiven me. Thank God!"

Introduction

Is your approach to your relationship with your wife working as well as you would want? If you want to see significant improvement, wouldn't you try anything that gets good results? It is my belief that the reason most men give up or fail at relationships is not because they lack the desire to make it work. It is because they don't have a plan that works and have given up trying.

About 4 years ago, my wife, Rita and I were in an argument. I was letting her know what she was doing wrong in our relationship, and what she needed to do to fix it. And that was that! Needless to say, she not only rejected my appraisal, but she also indicated she was not open to discussion on the topic. I remember being so mad, thinking, "What's wrong with her?" I left the conversation frustrated and dissatisfied.

Later that day I sensed God, that quiet inner voice, asking me a question. "How long have you been telling Rita exactly what's wrong with your relationship with her, then telling her how to fix it?" I responded in my mind, "25 to 30 years." Then another question came to mind, "Has it worked?" My answer was emphatically, "NO!" At the time, I didn't know what to do with that information. But my quest for another method began here.

In business, we know we need a plan to succeed. We recognize a goal, commit to go for it, decide on a strategy to accomplish it, and then put it into action. We know it works in our lives at work; why not apply this to our lives at home?

First, we need to recognize our goal. God said David was a man after His own heart. In 1 Samuel 13:14, Samuel spoke to Saul about David: "But now your kingdom will not endure; the Lord has sought out a man after his own heart and appointed him leader of his people, because you have not kept the Lord's command." Can we be men after our wife's own heart? I believe so, with a resounding "Yes!" What could your relationship look like if you made the commitment to be a man after your wife's own heart?

Here's the tough part. You say, "John, I've lost that loving feeling," and so have many others. The Righteous Brothers didn't sell millions of records to people who didn't relate to that saying — they hit a nerve. Let me assure you, it doesn't matter if you have lost your original, loving feelings toward your wife. You make the decision to love her based on a commitment to do it — not a feeling. Feelings change, commitment doesn't.

Let me share what I have learned about myself and other men. Once we make a decision to do something, we are relentless in pursuit of it. Men can be consumed with not letting a goal go. Our God given staying power, our nature to be driven, can be our greatest weakness when pushed to an extreme. But God also gave us this sense of drive for a reason. We can turn this weakness into strength when we commit to a worthy goal.

Your mind and emotions may cry out, "I can't. I don't feel loved, valued, or respected." I respond, "I know, but what you've been doing hasn't worked."

In October of 2003, I met the person who was the catalyst for this book. We met in the fitness center of our small town. Conversation quickly went to something meaningful, as my friend-to-be, Richard, explained a strategy that worked well for him in his goal of achieving financial success.

Richard challenged me: "You should choose a goal that would dramatically improve your life." At the time, I was searching for more meaning in my life. I was redefining my own personal significance, previously based on material things or accomplishments. So, I knew Richard's goal for financial success wasn't what I needed at the time. However, his challenge to choose a specific goal tugged at my heart for the rest of the day. After much prayer about it that evening, I woke up with the answer. I chose to apply these principles to a much different kind of goal.

The goal that I discovered in prayer that night was to improve my relationship with my wife of 35 years. I want the best possible relationship with Rita. And even though it was already good at this time, I wanted it to be great. I made the commitment to be a man after my wife's own heart.

The strategy I developed to accomplish this goal is what I now refer to as *The Ten*. I have been fully committed to applying *The Ten* for the last 18 months and I can assure you that this strategy works. In the upcoming pages there will be a variety of suggestions and stories that will help you understand each of *The Ten* steps. *The Ten* action steps are our "how-to-plan" to guide you as you follow through on your decision to improve your relationship with your wife. Let me say in all confidence, it's a simple program. But remember — *simple is not easy.*

Remember, you have a high calling of being a man/husband. Within all of us God has put into our fiber staying power. It has just been misapplied to the wrong goals.

Your new goal: To be a man after my wife's own heart.

Commit to God and to yourself to pursue this goal faithfully. Be committed to it. As Winston Churchill said in a commencement address at his former school in England, "Never give up. Never give up. Never give up."

You will find the strategy for pursuing this goal in the following pages. Ask the Lord to bless your efforts. Pray for the desire, motivation, and will to apply these steps. With Him all things are possible.

IMPORTANT:
Please keep in mind the following paradox when working this program. Sometimes the more we try in our own strength to change our self or influence others, the more we are frustrated by our inability to do it.

To overcome our character flaws and see real change in our behavior, sheer will power is not enough. The turning point for transformation is a balance between a surrendered life, repenting of our old destructive ways, and putting in the footwork.

When working each step you need to surrender your will and receive God's power. A suggestion you might try is a prayer similar to this.

"Lord, I can't do this in my strength, and I want to change. I need the power of the Holy Spirit to change my thinking and acting. I will do my part. Thank you for helping me".

May God bless your efforts abundantly.

John

How it works:

First and foremost you must not let your wife know what you are doing.

The excitement for you will come when you see the change in your relationship. Under no circumstances should you tell her, because it will lose its effect.

You will want to share your progress, so share it with a friend you can trust. I believe that this method will work best if you are not doing this alone. Do you have a good guy friend at church or work? You need someone you can trust and who can be a good encouragement to you. Commit to doing *The Ten* together and you can hold each other accountable as you stick to your goal and the program to accomplish it. If you don't have a friend who will commit to this goal with you, I encourage you to have a person to talk to like a pastor or counselor. Another person can be a great asset in helping you stay the course.

I've listed some questions at the end of each chapter to guide you in a discussion about each step, but they are just examples. I encourage you to answer them honestly on your own first. Then you can talk through them with your friend. They might lead to other questions or more discussion. Be honest with each other about your approach to each step and encourage each other to stay the course. Your friend may be confident at a step that you struggle with. Ask him for other examples of how to accomplish it. The goal is that this whole process becomes natural.

In each chapter you will be presented with a new step to apply to your relationship with your wife. These are action steps – you must take action. There are ten of them. Only one should be done each day. Throughout the entire day keep only that one step in mind.

I have found the easiest way for me to remember what step I am on: I line up the dates with the steps. The best way to start the plan is on the first, 11th, 21st, or 31st day. To follow this system, take the last number of the date and do that step. If it is the 11th of the month, start with Step 1; the 12th of the month, start with Step 2. If it is the 21st of the month, start with Step 1; the 22nd of the month, start with Step 2; and so on. Within a 30-day month you will work each step three times. This is a perpetual program: you are continually doing one step each day.

Please keep this in mind as you work the program. Sometimes the suggestion for the day might not be practical for that particular day. You might be away on business and unable to do the required step for the day, or just unavailable to do it because of your schedule or your wife's schedule. My suggestion for these days is to take a day for planning. Think about what things you could do over the weekend or when you have the opportunity to follow through with the step. Don't let it pass by without focus on the particular step for the day.

Also, after you've put The Ten into practice for five or six months, you will find yourself thinking of all of the steps all the time. You will discover that you are less critical each day and compassionate more of the time. To start off with, don't try to tackle all the steps in one day. Focus on one and be very intentional with that step that day.

In the back of this book is a list of *The Ten*. I would suggest you make a copy and keep it with you in your wallet.

I encourage you to look at your list each morning, memorize your step for the day, and then do it throughout the day.

I believe these are the three most difficult challenges in doing this Program:

1. Don't forget to look at the step for the day every morning.
2. When you feel emotionally needy and want to go back to your old behavior — don't.
3. Don't be discouraged by the amount of time it takes before you see improvement in your relationship. Just keep on keeping on. The good feelings will follow the actions you are about to start.

Closing comment: You only have one wife. On a scale of 1 to 10, rate your relationship now. We will revisit it at the end of this book.

Chapter 1 — Listen to her
(Days 1, 11, 21, 31)

The first time I recognized and acknowledged the power of listening, I wasn't thinking of using it at home, but more for its application in business. Formerly, my company would send its employees to a training seminar each year. Here we would learn to improve our negotiating skills, planning, team building, etc. One session was a listening seminar, geared to help talkative sales people become better listeners. I was intrigued but skeptical. I was in my mid-40s and I believed in persuasive communications (my wife might call it manipulative communications). I really believed that when I used subtlety and timing in my job as a salesman, I could affect a result. There is some degree of truth in this; however, my focus was usually on the points *I* wanted to make. I heard a problem and gave "the" solution. I didn't know to do anything differently.

At this seminar we were presented with an exercise: listen, then repeat your client's statements back to them. For example, your client informs you of a quality problem: "John, what's wrong with your plant? Their poor quality created big problems for us — lines slowed down, production quotas can't be met, and I'm the one who gets called to fix the problem or change suppliers. This can't go on." In the seminar we learned to do the following: "Joe, what I hear you saying is that our poor quality has created numerous problems — down time, slow production, missed quotas, and angry production managers who are demanding you fix it and do it fast." As simple as this repetition seems, it does communicate to your client you have listened to them.

After the seminar, I flew home to our 175-year old farm-house in a great country setting. This home has been very special to our family for many years. My wife, Rita, has been the manager of a high-end fabric and furniture store for seven years. For those of you non-retail people, let me tell you that it's very hard. You have no gatekeeper at that front door: you get the good, the bad, and the mean. You're on your feet a lot and today's retail customer gets more and more demanding and wants no problems.

That evening, I hugged Rita the way I usually do when I get home. As we were talking in the kitchen, she said some-thing like, "Today was so hard. I had two major reworks [custom work that had to be done over], unreasonable demands, and my feet are killing me." With all sincerity, I said, "It sounds like your day was filled with a lot of stress — from the reworks to demanding customers, and on top of that you're dealing with pain in your feet."

She looked at me stunned and said, "You were really listening?" You would have thought I had found the Rosetta Stone — the key to letting my wife know she was special to me. But what do I go and do? The very next day, I was back to my old ways of listening.

My good friend and pastor, Jim, once gave me this golden nugget. "A good question is far better than a right answer." As you continue reading this chapter, you will realize how difficult it is for me to not give answers. I like to help people (particularly my wife) by giving solutions and the answers. But Jim encouraged me to stop giving answers and start asking more questions.

You can begin to apply these techniques now. A great way to let your wife know you're involved in what she's saying is to ask questions. First clarify the information she's giving you by repeating back to her. Then ask questions about how she feels about what she's telling you about. For instance, "When that happened, how did that make you feel?" Then listen carefully and repeat what you heard. Next time you hear a good probing question, write it down, but most importantly, listen to her response!

I wasn't so quick in applying this information. Years after the listening seminar, I asked my friend (who is also a professional counselor) for a way to know my wife better. Vin knows my wife well and this information helped me a great deal. He said, "At the right time — and it needs to be right, quiet and focused, with no distractions — ask her, 'Can you tell me how I make you feel safe? How do I make you feel unsafe?' or, 'What do I do that gives you security? What do I do that makes you feel insecure?'" Well, I waited for the perfect moment and we had an insightful conversation.

She answered, "With the following you make it safe: I know you're reliable. What you say you'll do, you do. I feel safe because you're dependable and I can count on you. I feel unsafe when I share things that are important to me, you answer with quick-fix solutions. When you do that, I feel you must think I'm stupid because I couldn't see that. I don't want an answer; I just want you to listen. So I guess the way you make me feel unsafe or not valued is when you make it unsafe for me to share with you."

That was the last thing I thought I would hear. I didn't think it was good or bad, it was just different from my expectations. At the time she shared this with me, I had not come to the place where I believed in the power of listening. I also did not have the ability to stop helping by giving solutions. It took many more years.

Needless to say, sales people like me, have strong feelings on what they believe the answer to be. After selling for over thirty-five years, I have seen some of my own strong ideas fail. I have realized that one of my own character flaws is in the ability to recognize that there are other solutions. My answer is not always the best, and might even be the wrong solution.

When we give quick solutions to our wives, we are listening with our ears, without involving our hearts. Now stay with me — listening with your heart is not as difficult as it seems. If you are learning to speak another language it takes time, practice, and patience. Listening with your heart takes time, practice, and patience. There is no easy way to accomplish this, but it is possible and will change your life when you start doing it.

First let me say that all conversations don't need to be approached by listening with or speaking from your heart. For one, it would be difficult and draining. Most conversations need your attention, listening with a focus on what your wife is saying. These conversations are external — about simple things like meeting a couple for dinner, running errands, or listening to daily everyday occurrences. It is important to mention that focused attention is very important. I personally don't like it when I'm talking and the other person is busy doing something else. It communicates to me that what I'm saying isn't important to them. Focused listening can be accomplished when you set your mind to it and commit to doing it.

The real difficulty for men is listening with your heart. Let me share a story to illustrate what I mean by this. Rita has told me many stories about difficulties at her store — everything from difficult remakes to difficult customers. We've had conversations over the years about hiring, firing, fun times and difficult times. Naturally, there were those times I would ask if she wanted my input. Most of the time, she said no, and I got used to that. Mostly I just listened. She presented these difficulties in a mild tone that was not filled with any serious concerns about what she was doing. Yes, retail is difficult. She knew that and accepted it.

As time went on, especially in this past year, I noticed more specifics in our conversations. As she would share, I made note of the big issues. These were the ones that were repeated more and more often. Our conversations regarded her work, our new grandson, and some health issues she was working through. It started to get my attention.

As she would share, I tried to see what she was feeling by looking at these big topics through her eyes. As I would do this, it touched my heart and almost brought tears to my eyes. Men, I hope the following might help you. Between the words, I heard that she would love to spend more time with Elias, our grandson. Also, she wanted to be more available when friends needed her. She wanted us to be able to do more things together, especially on a moments' notice, like visit our sons and their wives in Chicago and Boston. As I saw these conversations through her eyes, I realized those were the issues of her heart and I needed to do something.

One morning early in 2005, we drank coffee and talked in our usual spot in the living room. She told me that this would be her last year working; she wanted to retire at the end of December. I think she was prepared for me to respond negatively, but I didn't. I had already heard her heart's cry for several months. I just said, "Okay. Let's start working out how we make that transition." You might tell me that my wife retiring early shouldn't be a big deal, but it was for me. This came at the end of my working career, and a few more years of Rita working could make a significant financial difference for our future. But I have to say that her well-being means a lot more to me than the monetary income she brings into our home. This was no-brainer for me. I told her that I was 100% behind her decision.

The next time your wife brings up the same topic, don't tune her out because you think you've heard it before — listen carefully. If it's a subject that's troubling her, try to see it through her eyes and allow your heart to be touched.

Before you share your observation with her, ask the Lord for insight. Be open and willing to accept what she's saying between the words. Most women have a high threshold for pain, so don't let it go too far before you respond. I've heard many men who didn't see or hear the warning signals of a disaster. Don't be one of them.

When listening with your heart, it also means you should respond with grace. When you have seen the situation through her eyes, think about how you would want someone to respond to you. You will never go wrong by showing grace and compassion.

As men, we tend to build strong walls around our hearts. We can't listen or speak from our hearts with this wall in the way. It's time to drop your defenses, be vulnerable and open, and take the risk of exposing what you really feel. I encourage you to do this in a safe environment or you might get hurt and discouraged from doing it again. First, I suggest that you try it with your encourager and accountability partner for this book. You can be supportive of each other as you learn to listen and speak from the heart. Then take the chance with your wife. You might be surprised at her response.

I remember the first time I dropped my defenses with Rita. I had been at the top of sales in my company for over fifteen years. My company even gave me a plaque that said "Salesman of the Century." But two years after receiving this plaque, my sales plummeted and continued to be down for more than three years. I can't express the feelings I experienced, but I felt powerless over the drop. If you're like me, you know that I doubled all my efforts. I had great creative concepts, meetings with all the right people, but nothing happened. I felt stripped down to nothing as deal after deal went south.

One particular week, I had been working on five separate large deals. I had spent between two and five months on each one and they were so close to being completed. Within this one week, I lost all five. Five great deals — full of hope and optimism, sales incentive and dollars — vaporized in five days.

One night shortly after this, I started to feel very anxious, hopeless, and fearful. I turned to Rita, and for the first time in our married life said, "Rita, I'm afraid, really afraid. And I don't know what to do any more." She put her hand on my shoulder and gently said, "It's okay. I love you. It's okay." An amazing thing happened. The anxiety lifted. My big bad secret of fear, exposed to my wife, was out in the open. And guess what? It lost its power over me. I was afraid, and it was okay!

Learning to listen and speak from your heart should not be confused with being overly honest. Remember, honesty without compassion is brutality. This is not your opportunity to tap into your bitter resentful side and tell your wife all the things you've been bottling up. My personal role model in sharing from His heart is Jesus. He listened and on many occasions spoke from His heart.

One example of Jesus listening and responding from His heart that always moves me is the story about Lazarus and his sisters, Mary and Martha. "Lord, the one you love is sick. When he heard this, Jesus said, 'This sickness will not end in death. No, it is for God's glory so that God's Son may be glorified through it.'" (John 11: 3-4)

The moment for me that Jesus really shows that He listens with His heart is when both sisters come separately to Him. Jesus focuses all His attention on each of them and He heard the cry of their hearts with their faith. Both cried to Him, "Lord, if you had been here, my brother would not have died." (John 11: 21 and 32) One stood, the other fell at His feet and wept because of their loss. He felt their sorrow so greatly that, "he was deeply moved in spirit and troubled... Jesus wept." (John 11:33, 35) Even though He knew the outcome, He felt their loss deep within His spirit. Jesus told Martha, "I am the resurrection and the life. He who believes in me will live, even though he dies; and whoever lives and believes in me will never die." (John 11:25-26) Because Mary and Martha believed, he raises Lazarus from the dead.

Just meditate on this. The creator of all things with a mission to save the world continually demonstrated His focused attention by being in the moment. He always responds with compassion and by revealing His heart to others.

What we speak from our mouths does reveal what's in our hearts. "For as he thinks in his heart, so is he." (Proverbs 23:7 - NKJV) If you don't like what's coming out of your heart there's only one way to change it. There's no pill, no surgery, no self-improvement plan – there's only God.

It's time to take action in the first step of *The Ten*. Start with attentive, focused listening for good practice. Listen carefully when your wife gives you details on dinner or picking up something on your way home from work. When you're together, stop what you're doing when she's talking and just listen. This has to be very intentional on your part. Don't offer solutions; just focus and listen. Remember, you had all the answers in the past. This is about valuing your wife with listening.

The next big step is to involve your heart in your listening process. Get honest with God and tell Him what you're trying to do. He will help you to get reacquainted with your heart again, your core. He loves to do heart renovation. He can take down the walls around your heart, but He needs your willingness. Remember, focused and attentive listening with your ears is only part one. The next step is learning to listen from and speak with your heart and only God can help.

God is still the same yesterday, today, and tomorrow. He will be the One to change your heart. He's a wonderful listener and wants you to become one also. God's key objective is to make us more and more like Christ. Jesus was a wonderful listener. He touched the lives of others, and He heard their words as well as the emotions behind them. That's what he wants us to do: listen with our ears and our heart.

Study Questions
Chapter 1 – Listen to Her

1. What are some of the things you can do when your wife is sharing with you?

2. Is there a difference between hearing and listening?

3. Write down at least 3 good questions you can ask her when she is talking. (Ex: "When that happened, what did you think or how did that make you feel?")

4. What does making your wife feel secure mean to you? Do you know how you do this or don't do it?

5. What do you think will be the biggest challenge for you in this chapter?

6. Pray about who the Lord would want to be your accountability partner as you work these steps. Please have your partner by the next chapter. It will help your success.

Chapter 2 – Value Her: She's a Priority
(Days 2, 12, 22)

When I was nineteen, I had a job and went to college at night. I was looking for a car and my father was helping me out. My dad worked in a restaurant and the owner of the nearby used car dealership ate there a lot. He started to tell my dad about good cars and good buys when they came in. When I got the call from my father about a car in great shape, I met him that night to look it over. You can imagine my surprise and excitement when I saw this 1958 Corvette, in mint condition with all the features. I can still close my eyes and visualize this beautiful baby blue convertible Vette in the showroom. I bought it that night. Talk about valuing something.

My wife, who was my girlfriend back then, once reminded me how over the top I was with that car. It was always clean, shining, well serviced and always in the garage. I wanted to preserve that new car smell as long as I could, so nobody even smoked in it. The funny thing is that several times as an adult, I have dreamed that I never sold it: that its been in my parents' garage and it's still mine, even though my parents haven't lived in that house for over thirty years. The value I placed on that car was extremely high. As I look back now, I can see how much that car meant to me. My care of it was very intentional: it was a priority.

That's what I mean when you consider Step 2 – *Value Your Wife: She's a Priority.* The ability to make a decision to value your wife and to follow through with it is something a man was made for. Our ability to value something in that way has just been directed toward other things.

God shows us His value of us through His unconditional love and grace. He wants to duplicate this unfailing love in each man. I know that seems like a big task, but God wants to help you. The great thing about God's grace and love is that you will receive it when you ask for His help. When we talk about value, it has to be sandwiched between unconditional love and grace: love that acts kindly with the grace that forgives. We were created to show our wife and children that our love will endure.

We have the greatest example of one who valued others on earth – Jesus. He was the master at giving value to those who never got it. Remember the story of the woman about to be stoned? Jesus found Himself in the middle of a setup with self-righteous men and a woman who had been trapped in a mistake. Jesus knelt and wrote in the dirt some truths that exposed the hearts of these men. Each man dropped his stone and walked away.

When Jesus looked up from his writing, only the woman remained. He asked her, "Woman, where are they? Has no one condemned you?" "No one, sir," she said. "Then neither do I condemn you," Jesus declared. "Go now and leave your life of sin." (John 8:10-11) What a great example of imparting value. Jesus was the living act of God's demonstration of value and this woman learned a valuable lesson on grace. She had encountered a man who didn't condemn her for her actions, but restored her value in few words. Remember, if Jesus went to the cross for you, and He did, there is no excuse not to go the distance for your wife.

I had the opportunity to show this kind of love and grace in a father-son program I formerly led. For nineteen years,

I worked in a program for five- and six-year-old boys and their dads. Our motto was "we don't separate the men from the boys." We always paired up a little boy with a man when his father wouldn't participate or if he didn't have a dad who could come. We met once a week for an hour and a half: thirty minutes for a fun sports-type activity; thirty minutes for a cool craft; and thirty minutes of good stories with character lessons, then some prayer time.

There was one little boy – let's call him Bobby — who was probably one of the most difficult little boys I've ever had. One night during story circle time, I felt someone pushing on my back. Little Bobby was using a magic marker to draw on my new sweater. When I realized what was going on, I turned to him, looked him right in the eye and said, "Bobby, there isn't anything you could do to stop me from loving you." He just looked at me and smiled.

After about three months, Bobby waited for everyone to leave one of our meetings so he could ask me a question. "Ranger John, each Friday morning at my school we have show-and-tell. Would you be my show-and-tell?" Before I could respond, he continued and told me, "I know you like me, I can tell. The kids at school don't like me and treat me bad. If you were to come to my class and tell them that you like me, I know they would listen to you. Please, will you come?" I said the only thing a Ranger could say, "Sure, just have your mom call me." She did and arranged it with the teacher.

My big day arrived. Let me first tell you what I do as a professional. I create, market, and sell kids' stuff that ends up in happy meals, cereal boxes, and kid-type consumer products. I spent several hours on the presentation for Bobby's class. I put together thirty kits with all kinds of neat stuff: from 3-D glasses to puzzles we did for a cereal company. I introduced myself as Ranger John and explained that Bobby was a good friend of mine in our Tree Climber Club and that he had asked me to make a presentation at his school.

I divided the class into two groups – McDonald's toy testers and Burger King toy testers. Then I presented the fun stuff I had brought for all of them. Their task was to decide as a group which toy they would choose for the next promotion. We all had a great time. Bobby became a legend because he knew the guy that made the toys that McDonald's, Burger King, and others gave out. As I got to my car after leaving the class, I bowed my head and thanked God that He allowed me to be Bobby's show-and-tell. I heard a small voice say "You are all my show-and-tells. Show the world what I have done for you, then tell them." I have never forgotten that lesson.

You can think about valuing your wife like a show-and-tell. Show her your affection and let your actions show her that she's a priority. In *Step Four* we will talk more about the speaking part, but now I want to talk about showing her that you value her by your actions. I would like to address two very important parts in this: the external part and the internal part. The external part is what you do – the action – that shows her she is valued.

Our actions can either add or take away value from our wives. It is similar to the concept of *Sell value not price*. I am a value selling sales person. What does it mean to sell value? It means there is more to an item than just the price. The real benefits of a new concept or idea are worth a lot more than any price.

For over 25 years, one of my best customers was Mike. He was the exclusive licensing representative for the Major League Baseball Players Association and one of the best salesmen I knew. Mike used to tease me by calling me 10% Johnny. He told me that he knew he paid me at least 10% more than my competitors, but it was well worth it.

Mike told me about a company that visited him to take a look at what we had produced for him. Without any hesitation, they told him that they could produce everything I did and save him a minimum of ten percent. Mike then told them that he didn't need them to save money on what's been done, but to create things that have never been done before. He told them that my company had made him very wealthy with our innovation and creativity. He didn't need a cost cutter; he needed an idea maker. Ten percent was a small price for that.

Just as it is difficult to put a price tag on an idea, there is no way to measure the value of your wife. As easy as it is to have the value we bring to our customers discounted by them, we do the same to our wives if we bring that attitude home. What I'm going to say might offend some of you, and it might not apply to others of you. If it doesn't apply, don't take it. Just like companies cut overhead, we see our wives as overhead. We think we must somehow do to her what is done to us professionally – strip her of her value. Any way you can reduce the time you spend with her or the money you spend on her, you do. The net result is that she feels that she is of no value. Your actions and words communicated it. Are you a value stripper of your wife? Be honest.

Do you look for opportunities to point out her shortcomings, her weaknesses, or character flaws? Well, stop it! It's as simple as that. Stop doing that. As you diminish her, your stock does not go up in value. In fact, both of your stocks go down.

One day Rita and I were having a rough time. I was about to take her inventory: show her each of the ways she was lacking. Before I went down that slippery road, God intervened. A small, gentle thought came into my head, "How many years have you been trying to change her with that approach?" My thought was, "A long, long time." The next thought, "Has it worked?" My answer was a resounding, "No, of course not!" Thankfully I did not start down that road in my conversation with Rita. I stopped and prayed, "Lord help me. I know it's more about me than about what's wrong with her. *I* need to be fixed." I'm sure this list of *The*

Ten was an answer to my prayer that day because it wasn't long after that moment that I discovered this method and started putting it into practice.

How do we stop stripping our wife's value? It starts by regaining our own. We can't rely on what our wives feel or think about us to give us value. And we certainly can't make her think or feel the way we want her to about us. We regain our value by what we do and say to our wives. It comes when we see her as a valued partner.

Now that I have stopped trying to manipulate Rita to love or respect me, I see her true value. I can see what she brings to our marriage and it's a lot more than ten percent. I've seen her incredible determination to value our family by her actions. She gives her time, money, and strength to our sons and their wives. She has forgiven me of some very unforgivable actions. Tom Cruise in *Jerry McGuire* said, "You complete me." In our marriage Rita not only completes me, but in our family she makes us all better than we would be.

Think about this for a while. Make a list of the things that your wife does that you hate to do. It takes a tireless effort to build a relationship. Always look for the good in your wife. When you see the negative, let it go – it's a bad habit. Redirect yourself to look for the good.

Letting go of these negative actions will improve your marriage greatly. But the positive actions we can take will add even more value to our wives. A demonstration of this will not be cheap. It's not about flowers on Valentine's Day. It's not about a great trip or dinner out on your anniversary. It's not about getting her an expensive birthday present, even though all of these are good and I encourage you to be thoughtful on special dates. What I'm talking about is bigger than that. It's choosing to value her everyday.

Do you know how aware a woman is? Do you realize the subtle actions or gestures they can pick up on, especially when it comes to their husbands? Your wife is keenly aware of what turns your head and what grabs your attention. She might never mention it, but she knows it. Your actions reveal a lot about your heart.

Your actions can first change mostly in the little things: open doors for her, look at her from a distance, or have your face light up when you see her. When I first started applying this step, I would put down the newspaper or book or turn off the TV and give Rita eye contact. When we would talk or she asked me a question, I would stop what I was doing and listen to her. Any of these things are possible when you decide to do them. Make the commitment to try these new actions on *Day Two*.

Now that we've talked about your external behavior to demonstrate value to your wife, it's time to take a look at internal behavior. The internal part is what goes on in your mind when she's there and when she's not. This part is going to be painstakingly difficult. I believe as a man thinks, so he is. Valuing her in your thoughts will be a challenge that will pay huge dividends when you learn to do it.

The man who had the cleaning contract for our office once told me that because his wife was overweight, he had the right to dream, think, and lust for other women. He told me that the things that went on in his mind didn't hurt anybody. I responded gently that it did hurt someone — it hurt him. Every time he thought about another woman, he was reinforcing to himself that he got the short end of the deal. Each time he made that comparison in his mind, he was the loser. He was causing himself anger, resentment, and self-pity because of his stinking thinking.

In 2001, I went back into a twelve-step program. I am a big advocate of the twelve-step process. Step four is *The Inventory Step*, where we, in as much self-honesty as possible, see some real patterns. In step five we humbly admit to God, ourselves, and someone else, the exact nature of our wrongs. In step six we become more aware of our shortcomings; and in step seven, humbly ask God to remove all the defects of our character.

When you complete each of the steps, there are many wonderful miracles that take place. The amazing thing is that as I'm made aware of my shortcomings, my awareness increases to the point that I can't ignore them any more. There was a time that I was made aware of what would catch my eye, and where my thoughts would go from there. Shortly after being made aware of this habit, I wanted it to stop. The more I tried to stop looking, the worse it got. When I shared this with a friend and confessed this to God, something good happened. I can't explain how He did it, but my desire to let my eyes wander left me when I realized that I was powerless to make myself stop. God's power came in and He took away the desire to look. Later, He replaced it with a desire to look and think about my wife. He gave me His eyes to see her differently. I quit seeing her as my roommate, and started seeing her as a gift from Him. Start by asking God to help you make your wife, not someone else, the apple of your eye.

God will help you stop devaluing the one He gave you to value the most. We are men and we are not capable of such change on our own. If you're reading this book it's no accident. God is going to change you from the inside out. Your part is to confess to Him and another person what you have been doing in your mind. "Therefore confess your sins to each other and pray for each other so that you may be healed." (James 5:16) It still works. This process is both external and internal.

Let me end this step with one last story. About 17 years ago, Rita and I were going through a difficult time. I, as usual, was in a place of being needy and Rita didn't want to fix or address it. I had the tendency to try to trap her with my words and put her in a very emotionally unsafe place. Out of frustration and to inflict more pain, I finally said,

"Maybe we should just end it – get a divorce." I will never forget her response.

Her detached eyes became very focused into mine. She said, "I never, never, ever want to hear you say that again. I will not give my family a legacy of a broken marriage. We are two smart adults. We can figure this out." She was right, we did.

You see, Rita's object of value was far greater than mine – the legacy of our family. She placed a high value on us and was willing to do whatever it took to make it work. Men, we need that kind of tenacity. It is too easy for us to be influenced by others and ourselves. If God has the power to raise the dead, He can certainly raise a dead marriage if you let Him. For your sake, let Him.

Study Questions:
Chapter 2 – Value Her:
She's a Priority

1. Name some people places or things you valued growing up.

2. What would be the first thing you can do to make your wife a priority? When can you start?

3. When you were a child, what did show and tell mean? What does it mean today in regard to this step *Value her – She's a priority*?

4. List some ways people strip value from each other. Have you ever done that with your wife? Describe ways you have stripped value of her.

5. How do you add value to your wife?

6. When you look for the good, what do you see? List at least 7 qualities.

7. When you compare your wife to other women, in your mind what are you really doing?

8. Pick a time with your accountability partner when you can meet a minimum of once every two weeks. With at least one call per week.

Chapter 3 — Spend time with her: She's a priority
(Days 3, 13, 23)

What is the most precious thing we have that we can give to anyone? Time! What a concept. At one of my twelve-step meetings someone shared that they had spent their life trying to *make* time. Then one day they came to understand that they couldn't make time, they had to *take* time — take the time and use it.

Have you ever had someone invest time in you? From age twenty-two to thirty-one, I worked in New York City and became our company's youngest sales manager in this highly competitive area. At that time, I had no faith and no God in my life. I remember saying many times in jest, "I pray that there's not a God, 'cause if there is, I'm in deep trouble." The irony is that after years of relying only on myself, I got into deep trouble. My world started to crumbled. At thirty-one, I was at the top of my business game with a lot of material success. Then I was hit with fear, anxiety, and a sense of failure. It started in February of 1976 and lasted almost fifteen months. Thank God the greatest intensity lasted only the first four months.

After a vacation with my family, I hit my lowest point. God intervened and revealed His grace to me, but my recovery would still be a long process. At the time I had to take a lot of pills, which I hated to rely on. I also went to see

37

a very good counselor that God used to help me make the right choices.

During this fifteen-month journey to Jesus, my friend Mike called me. Mike was a client who had become a good friend — almost like a brother. Outside of business, we would get together often because we had a lot in common. Our wives had also become good friends. Well, Mike was a fitness guy and was always in great shape. One afternoon after a meeting at his office he said, "Next Tuesday, meet me at my gym." We got together for about an hour every Tuesday from then on during that tough year. Mike coached me in my workout and pushed me hard. He didn't like seeing me depressed, with lack of zeal, and he wanted to change that. He was especially relentless about getting me off my medication. He just wouldn't let up on me. Then each week, after we worked out, we would go to a great Irish restaurant to have our favorite crab legs, a baked potato, and a cold beer.

At the time I didn't know how important this was in the beginning of my recovery. Mike made a commitment to me that cost something — time. His job was one that called for lots of extra time and travel, but he never missed a Tuesday with me. When I needed someone, Mike was there. Years later, I think of him very dearly as my model for investing time in someone. Can I be that Mike to the person who needs me? My wife and children are a great place to start.

How can you invest time in your wife? Know what she likes to do and do it with her. Somewhere in my past, I heard the following, "Because Jesus went to the cross for you, you can surely go to the mall with your wife." Now I have never liked the sound of this but the principle is true. Jesus went to the cross for you and me and was obedient unto death. Is God asking you to be obedient to death in your relationship? In a way, yes! "Husbands, love your wives, just as Christ loved the church and gave himself up for her." (Ephesians 5:25) He died for the church and demonstrated how to be a servant to others here. We are to use His model in our relationship with our wives.

Spending time with your wife shows her that she's a priority. When I started to practice this third step, I learned that Rita loves to visit museums, old estates, and do things that are somewhat cultural. When she started to plan these day trips for us, she wanted them to be special — and they were. One of our first visits was to the Rockefeller estate in New York State. It was great: she loved it and I became more interested in J. D. Rockefeller. Also, it was a real vacation for me — an escape from doing lawn and outside work. We spent time together touring the estate, then had a late lunch at a little Greek restaurant. I still remember how nice it was for it to be just the two of us eating and talking at an outdoor table. It was a very special day.

Another way to spend time with your wife is to invest in a small community of other couples. I am so thankful that soon after becoming Christian, my wife and I were invited to be part of something very new to us. In 1979, a couple from Indiana came to our church in Connecticut and started the first small group. They prayed and picked five couples from our church, and we were one of those couples. As I look back, this group was perfect. We had many friends outside of church, but as we wanted to grow more in our relationship with Jesus, we also longed for new friends with whom we could share our new journey of faith. This new group was God's answer.

The friends we made in that small group were deeper and more real than any other friendships we had experienced. We were able to share similar concerns and discuss them in order to discover God's solutions. This small group met every two weeks and it became a high priority for Rita and me. Our commitment was if we were in town and well, we would be there even with three young boys at home. It was a big part of our life together. It also filled a void for Rita who wanted to have closer friends with whom she could share more intimate details. Almost twenty-five years later we are still very close to these friends.

I've heard many excuses by men on why they are not involved in these kinds of groups. The excuses are really an attempt to cover-up their fear of intimacy. The reality is that most of us don't know how to verbalize our feelings, so we just continue in the comfort of what we know: relationships that lack true intimacy. We also tend to build walls around our hearts so that no one can see through us or affect our emotions. As difficult as it might be for you to go to a small group, I encourage you to give it a try. There have been many times when I got involved in a something new. At first I felt inadequate, anxious, and unsure, but after time of being committed to it, the results were great.

There are many wonderful dividends to being involved in a small group. The people in your group can become your most trusted friends because of your investment in each other and commitment to be there for each other. Jesus was the king of community. He created it, modeled it, and lived it. His disciples were His trusted friends whom He shared His life with. When trust is developed among members of your small group, honest sharing can take place. It is important for your wife to have events or small groups where she has a safe place to voice her thoughts, ideas, and concerns. Even more important, she needs to know that this is a priority to you. You can demonstrate this to her by being involved in a group like this with her.

Rita and I now have a thiry-year history of small groups and we certainly have been exposed to some great studies. One series that comes to mind when I think of demonstrating your priorities with your time is *Hidden Keys to Loving Relationships* by Gary Smalley, a twelve-part video series. There's a part where Gary Smalley does a skit with a plant called Ivy. Ivy looked sick, neglected, and almost dead. He said that Ivy needed water, sun, and good soil. He used this as an analogy to demonstrate that if we wanted our marriages to grow, they needed to be nurtured and made a priority. While watching this video, one of the women in our group had to leave in tears. She was struck with ways that her husband would prioritize so many things ahead of her. Her wound was deep and the tears flowed.

If you are serious about making your wife a priority, then do what you can to fulfill her needs without thinking about yourself. This step of obedience is about her and your relationship with her. It may start by joining a small group together.

Maybe you have some serious issues or problems that need to be resolved in a more personal setting. This could take place more effectively outside of a group. One time when our marriage hit a low point it was clear to me that Rita had lost that loving feeling toward me. She just closed down emotionally and this made me even angrier. Thankfully, during this time we were in counseling. Our counselor, Vin became one of Rita's biggest fans and she his, but it wasn't until much later that I also learned to appreciate him. Each week we met with him separately for thirty minutes each. This initial separateness worked out well for us because it gave Rita the safety she needed to share some of her inner-most feelings when she wasn't ready to trust me with them. During those sessions, I got so angry with Vin because it seemed that most of the hard work of change in our relation-ship was on me. In hindsight I can see how right he was and how immature I was. He was calling me to become a man and I wanted to stay a boy. I thank God for his patience with me to complete this process.

Today I repeat my lesson to men I meet with — making men out of boys is not easy. Most of us would never admit to acting like a boy. Denial runs deep, but spend a few minutes and look over your life. Is it filled with grown-up boy activities? Or are there more examples of pouring some of yourself into others?

Before I move on from the benefits we received from counseling, I need to address this issue one more time. One of my friends who is a solid Christian and involved in many good activities, has made it perfectly clear to his wife that he will never go to a counselor. I know this grieves her because there are some issues that will never get addressed, let alone resolved. Don't ever turn away from counseling. God wants to speak into our lives and counseling is one tool He can use to speak to us. One of the first acts of humility is admitting that you don't have all the answers and you need help. Nothing but pride keeps one from seeking help — false pride. You might have some real concerns or secrets that a counselor could help you work through. It is no accident that you are reading this book. This could be your first step in admitting that you need some help.

Every step takes a first step. In twelve-step work, one step is about admitting to God, yourself, and another human being the exact nature of your wrongs. If you have some things in your life that you're doing or ashamed of, consider seeing a friend, pastor, or counselor you can trust. The scripture is very clear about confessing your sins with each other so you will be healed. "Therefore confess your sins to each other and pray for each other so that you may be healed." (James 5:16) In twelve-step work they say, "You're only as sick as your secrets." Satan's strategy is to keep you trapped in captivity with your shame and guilt. Jesus' plan for your life is to set you free. Whatever you need to do, do it. Make a call, see a friend, and take that risk. It's the only way you will be free.

If you sense that Satan holds you captive in this kind of shame and guilt, how many more chains will your children inherit as your legacy is passed down? You can decide the kind of legacy you want to give to your children. Think back over your family of origin, especially the men in your family and the relationships they had with their wives. Are there cycles that you need to break? If isolation, lack of trust, the blame game, or resentments are there, you can end it here. Be the man who breaks the cycle. It starts by admitting that you can't do it alone, then seeking help.

Bring this to the Lord in prayer. Ask Him to put on your heart the person you need to see to start this process. Then call and make an appointment. It would be great for you to become willing to go with your wife and get help together. Whatever it takes for you to get there, do it. There is a saying that you have to get heavy before you get light. Do the hard work in your relationship and it will become easier and easier.

I know what you're thinking… sometimes these suggestions won't be practical on day three. You're saying, "But John, what if we have our small group meeting on Monday, counseling on Thursday, and the 23rd of this month falls on a Tuesday? It's not like I can take a day off work every ten days and have a special planned day with her." That's true, this wouldn't be practical. You might be away on business and unable to do the required step for the day or it might not work with your schedule. I would encourage you to spend some time focused on the step for the day, no matter what. You could use a Tuesday as a planning day for a special day coming up or brainstorm about other ways you could spend time together.

Also, keep in mind that after about five or six months, you will start to integrate these steps into your life and you will find yourself doing all the steps all of the time. But to start off with, stay focused on the idea for the day. Plan, brainstorm, spend time with her after dinner, or talk for a while on the phone. You will think of something when you put your mind to it.

For example, if you were to ask my wife how she likes to spend time with me, one place she would mention is outside under our maple tree. The maple is a tree she and my sons planted over twenty years ago and it now stands forty feet tall. We have a few comfortable chairs and some tables under it. After a hard day at work, we sit down with a cup of coffee and sometimes a cookie and we reflect on the day. We have discussed a lot under that tree. In a way, we have grown up like the tree. Spending time together does not have to be complicated. In fact, I have found that the best times are the simplest: moments when I can just listen.

Recently a good friend of mine, who had a very special relationship with his wife, experienced the pain of seeing her die. After fifty-two years of marriage, she was diagnosed with a severe type of cancer and battled this disease for two years. My friend was with her almost all the time for those two years. His son told me about her last moments on earth before Glory. His father stroked his mother's forehead and told her that she was his beautiful, wonderful wife whom he loved with all his heart. She passed on and his son now has these memories of his father's unfailing love of his mother.

How did you learn to be a husband and father; was this role taught or caught? For most of us, we caught our lessons by observation — and lessons like my friend gave his son about love are rare. When I was growing up, I learned almost all of life's lessons by watching and hearing others.

My family didn't celebrate Christmas in a traditional way. Rita still finds it difficult to believe, but we opened presents way before Christmas. The religious element was not there either; we didn't go to church. We spent Christmas day at my Italian grandmother's house and had great food — antipasto platters, pasta, chicken, roast beef, fruits, cannoli — a feast!

Rita's family also had great food, but they included a religious element. She and her sisters went to church and presents were opened on Christmas day, not a week before. I caught a new way of Christmas from Rita's family. My wife brought her family's tradition of Christmas with her into our marriage. That has made the Christmas holiday very special at our home. We decorate the house very festively, invite friends and family to parties, and make sure Jesus stays the main focus of the time.

As a father, your children catch a lot of what you do. If you are a Christian and you want a legacy of a faithful marriage, you need to put *The Ten* into practice. I heard the following on a Christian radio station when a counselor from Texas shared what he had learned during twenty-five years of counseling. I want to share it with you because it is life changing and profound.

This counselor's specialty was working with adolescents. Usually a parent or couple would call him to set up an appointment for their child. He would always say, "If you want me to see your child, I first want to meet with both parents for four sessions." That was his criteria. Then he told the radio audience that he would ask the couple two questions.

"How often do you hold or touch your each other non-sexually in front of your children? How often does your child see the affection that you have for each other?" Next he would ask, "How many times a day do you say endearing things or compliment each other in front of your children?" Not to his surprise, most answers were little to none. He would then give them an assignment for the next two weeks. Hug or touch non-sexually in front of your children and say at least five endearing things or compliments to each other. For example, "That was a great meal!" or "You look great in that color." He said that in twenty-five years of counseling, most couples returned the following session to report that their child improved his or her behavior and this counselor was not needed.

That spoke to me. I felt like that was something easy that I could do. I made a decision to hug my wife when I got home and always compliment her in front of the boys on her great meals and other things. As I got wiser in our marriage, I would point out her gifts to our sons such as her good people skills and generous spirit. If you want your children to care for their husband or wife in the future, you need to demonstrate this kind of tender love to your wife in front of them.

When you can take the time to make your wife a priority, it means a great deal to your entire family. Do the right thing, put the time in even if you don't feel like doing it. You can even feel negatively, but just do what you know is right and the feelings will catch up. I have learned this so well over the years. During forty-one years of marriage, there were a number of times when the feelings were not there. If I hadn't known this principle, I would have been lost.

Believe it or not, love is not a feeling. Love can give you a good feeling, but don't rely on your feelings to make decisions. As a matter of fact, many of you might be at that spot right now where you have no feelings, or very little for your wife. This is the time when the real decisions happen. Anybody can make positive decisions when you *feel* good. The man you need to be makes good decisions when there are no feelings or even negative ones. When you do the right thing consistently — no moaning, no self-pity, no complaining — the good feelings will follow.

"Love is patient, love is kind. It does not envy, it does not boast, it is not proud. It is not rude, it is not self-seeking, it is not easily angered, it keeps no record of wrongs. Love does not delight in evil but rejoices with the truth. It always protects, always trusts, always hopes, always perseveres. Love never fails." (1 Corinthians 13:4-6) For some it will be easy, for others, it will be more difficult. It is harder if either of you grew up in a hurting family. God is a great source of strength.

Please remember that you cannot change her. You are powerless over her but not yourself. Ask God to help you grow and change. Ask the Holy Spirit to touch the areas in your life that need healing — even areas you don't know about. Give God permission to come into your life wherever He needs to. Only when your pain is addressed can you be free to love your wife generously.

I have been doing *The Ten* for over one and a half years. I must admit that my thoughts of Rita are sweeter and better. In the fall of 2005, we took a trip to Italy and we both spent time getting in better shape for it — more exercise so we wouldn't get tired too quickly. I find that now I want to live longer and feel better. Only God knows the moment I will take my last breath on earth, but I want to be healthy up to that point because I want to be there for Rita. I want to spend time with her and this only happened as a direct result of doing *The Ten* faithfully.

In the book of Proverbs, we are encouraged to make the best of each day. All through Proverbs, life is presented as many choices and acquiring Godly wisdom will help you choose wisely. In my youth, most of my choices were not based on Godly wisdom but worldly principles. The world teaches us to make choices based on self and to strive our own personal needs and desires. It's amazing that the more we try to please ourselves, the emptier we get.

Today you have a choice. Choose to love your wife. Remember that this choice is not based on a feeling, but is an act of obedience. God will honor your decision. Spending time with your wife demonstrates your commitment to be the man she needs.

Study Questions:
Chapter 3 — Spend time with Her:
She's a Priority

1. Name some of the things that your wife has suggested to do together. List the ones you did, the ones you didn't and why or why not.

2. What would be something that your wife would love to do? What would you need to do to make that happen?

3. How are you there for your wife? Name a time you demonstrated commitment.

4. Name some ways you can spend time with her that would make her notice.

5. What was said in this chapter that hit home with you? Explain.

6. What does your family history look like? How was caring/intimacy shown or not shown?

7. Do you say encouraging words to your wife or give her non-sexual hugs in front of your children? If not, dig deep into why.

8. If you need to improve in this area, make a plan and share it with your accountability partner.

Chapter 4 — Acknowledge Her Worth: Say It
(Days 4, 14, 24)

In my years working with men in business and church, I have learned many things about the way we think and act. One thing that holds true with all of us is that men want to feel their value appreciated and acknowledged before they are willing to give honest value in return. In the past, when I felt least valued, it was harder to be supportive of my wife and sons. When I sensed I had value, it was so much easier. So let's face it, it's not that hard to say something nice to our wives when we put our minds to it. You could start doing that without reading this chapter. However, I want you to change from the inside out. You can see her worth more easily when you understand your true value and where it comes from.

Here is the biggest area for you to personally grow. The fastest growing crime in America is also the fastest growing crime in the church: identity theft. Our identity of who we are in Christ is constantly in danger of being stolen. Following this kind of identity theft is theft of who we are as men. Satan wants to strip us of the manliness God wants in us. Do you realize that when your God given identity has been stolen, you also lose your authority as a man? Think of the consequences of not understanding who you are and not being able to take the authority you need to lead a family.

Let's think back about two thousand years. God sent his only son to free and liberate us from the bondage of sin and the works of Satan. Right after Jesus is baptized, the Holy Spirit leads Him into the wilderness. After forty days of fasting, Satan mounted a major attack on Jesus. The very first thing he said to challenge Jesus was, "If you are the Son of God, tell these stones to become bread." (Matthew 4:3) Please note that Satan's first attack was on Jesus' identity and remember that Satan is a student of man and a relentless foe. The fact that he went after Jesus' identity first proves our vulnerability in who we are. Satan's strategy hasn't changed in the past two thousand years; he tries to steal your identity first.

Your identity and value comes from who you are in Christ. Here are the facts when you receive Jesus Christ as your Savior.

1. You are of infinite value to God, which He declared by giving His Son's life for you. (1 Timothy 2:5-6)
2. God adopted you into His family. (Ephesians 1:4-6)
3. You are a child of God. (1 John 3:1)
4. Nothing can separate you from the love of God. (Romans 8:38-39)
5. You are unconditionally accepted by God. (Romans 15:7)
6. God is your guide (Psalm 119:105), provider (Matthew 6:28-32), healer (Matthew 14:14), counselor (John 14:26), friend (John 15:15), and Lord (Philippians 2:9-11)
7. You are completely forgiven of all sins. (1 John 1:9)
8. He wants you to be set free. (Romans 6:17-18, 2 Corinthians 3:17)

If you have any image in your mind other than what I've stated, your identity has been marred and potentially stolen.

Let me share one of my favorite allegories to help solidify this concept for you. About five hundred years ago, a king ruled a large kingdom and he had very specific laws.

One law stated that convicted thieves would be hung. The night before his execution, Robert—a convicted thief—waited in the dungeon for this sentence to be carried out. Early in the morning, four guards opened the door and shouted into the dungeon, "Robert!" Robert heard a voice across the cell respond, "I'm here." Robert didn't say a word as the guards covered the head of the voice they heard and led this man out.

The town gathered at the king's order to witness this execution because the king wanted to send a clear message of the price for stealing. The prisoner climbed up to the gallows with the covering on his head and the guards put the noose around his neck. The king read the crime and stated the sentence. When he finished speaking, the lever was pulled and the man died quickly. Then the king ordered the guards to cut the man down and remove the bag covering his face. When this was done, there was a loud moan from the people as they realized that the man who had been executed was the king's son.

The king immediately shouted, "Whoever is responsible for this will wish they had never been born." But just as he finished speaking, one of the guards found a note by his son's collar. The guard read aloud, "Father, please accept my life for the payment of Robert's crime." The king ran to the dungeon and opened the cell. He called in "Robert come out. You're a free man." As Robert came out, the king placed his arm around his shoulder, looked Robert in the eye and said, "Because my only son gave his life for you, your crime been paid for and you are free. The things that are in my kingdom are also yours to use. For if my son valued you so much that he gave his life for you, I will also value you because of my son's sacrifice."

Jesus didn't go to a gallows; He went to a cross to die for you. The Father accepts you, not because of what you did or didn't do but because of what His Son did. That's it. I encourage you to meditate on this fact so it can really sink in. The more you let this truth wash over you, the more things will change inside you. Once you can see the great value Jesus placed on you, you will feel valued and accepted. I know that for some of you, it might be the first time you truly experience this forgiveness. For others, it might be a familiar feeling to experience this truth and grace. The depth of who Jesus wants you to be can always be greater for any of us.

Tonight before you go to sleep, ask the Lord to open your heart and mind to receive all of what He accomplished on the cross. If you need to remind yourself of "Robert" every day until it sinks in, do it. You can't go back into the jail cell wanting to do something else for the king to earn your release. God paid for your release through the death of His son. Just accept it. What will happen as this reality sinks into your spirit? Your actions will have a pure motive. You won't try to gain God's acknowledgement or approval through your actions, but allow your actions to be a response to being loved unconditionally.

If you are still struggling with this concept, imagine this scenario. The king opens Robert's cell, calls him out, and lets him know his only son went to the gallows on his behalf — he is free. What if Robert had said, "Let me work your fields and clean your horses also. I feel the need to add something to the price your son paid so I might better deserve my release." Can you imagine the insult and stupidity Robert would have displayed? None of his little deeds could mean anything compared to the king's son's life. Many of us receive Jesus as Lord our Savior but we have trouble comprehending all of the implications. God is saying to you, "It's finished. Jesus paid the price for you. You are mine. It was my choosing, not yours, so don't try to add to my Son's work. Accept it and ask me how I want to use you."

As a husband, you are to value your wife like the king's son valued Robert — like Jesus values you. Let's now look at some ways you can do that. To the extent God has forgiven you and loved you, you are to do likewise with your wife and children. His glory is manifested by the way you respond with love to the wife and family He gave you. You did not deserve what was done on your behalf; you should now show others the same unconditional love. Can you grasp the freedom in that? You have no excuse not to show your wife the kind of love and forgiveness shown to you by Jesus. We are set free, so we must release others in return.

One of the hardest moments to demonstrate your value of your wife is in an argument or when you feel that you've been hurt and you feel like fighting back. Remember the attack Satan made on Jesus to threaten his identity? The third and last attack against Jesus is another example I want you to consider. Satan told Jesus he would give Him all the Kingdoms in the world if Jesus would bow down and worship him. Jesus, worship Satan?!?!

This tells us a lot about Satan and the battle we are fighting. God the Father and Jesus have not been separated in all eternity. In John 15, Jesus talks about the love that He and the Father have for each other and for us. It is humanly incomprehensible to know the depth of love the Lord Jesus has for the Father and us. Now, can you imagine that Satan — who has always seen the Godhead and watched this relationship — would think that Jesus would deny His Father and worship a mere created thing?

This shows us one of the many character flaws of Satan: he can't comprehend love. Unselfish love that doesn't require anything in return makes no sense to him. Maybe your marriage is on the rocks (maybe your wife or children have done hurtful things) and the voices in your head are screaming for you to hurt back, inflict hurt for hurt. At that crossroad—by the grace of God—you respond with compassion, acknowledge your mistakes, and ask for forgiveness. This is a response the evil one can't comprehend. He doesn't understand love. It takes him by surprise each time. Remember this the next time you want to respond to anyone by hurting back. Just say, "Hurt people, hurt people." God loves you. With His grace you can respond with love.

Once you start to feel that your true value comes from who you are in Christ, you won't be so dependent on your wife or success at work to give you value. At this point, you can discover the value and worth in those around you. Start by being a student again. Make it a point to learn about your wife and observe what she likes and dislikes. Listen to her express herself to learn her ways. You will find that the more you study your wife and the more you learn about her, your value for her will increase greatly.

Is there an area in your life that you really enjoy learning about? Is there a topic that you look forward to learning? I learn best by watching and listening, then read to supplement what I observe. I also ask questions of people who have more experience in a topic than I do.

In the months after I became a Christian, I developed a genuine interest in growing things, mostly vegetables. My interest continued to grow and I started to learn more and more. It all started with a few seeds on our sunporch, but their growth just fueled my passion. When I saw the results, I cleared a large section at the back of my property, cut down trees to open up the area to sunlight, and put up a four-foot fence with a sprinkler system. Even with this big garden in our back yard, my sunporch still looked like a miniature nursery. I read a lot of literature about planting and asked many questions of people who had productive gardens.

For a number of years, we had great vegetables —fresh tomatoes, lettuce, cucumbers, and carrots — and it was a lot of fun to see my hard work enjoyed by others at our dinner table. As a side bonus, the Lord would use my time in the garden to teach me valuable lessons. For example, if you stake a tomato plant to a pole early, it grows straight. If you keep tying it up, it will bear a lot of fruit. If you neglect the plant, it grows crooked, is very hard to correct and will not be a successful plant. A garden needs continuous care for many reasons — weeds, animals, and water — and if it is left unattended, it won't bear good results. In order to protect the plants from animals, I increased the height of the fence to keep deer out and extended it deeper into the ground to prevent woodchucks from going under the fence. I became a guardian of that garden.

In this same way, you are a guardian of your family. If you're traveling and spending many days away from your family (or garden), this is not a formula for success. In fact, you increase the odds for big problems with the most important people in your life. Subconsciously, you also might even be using your job as an escape from your real job at home. In the past thirty years, I have met many men that have great "lines" to justify many nights away from their family. If this is you, I would challenge you to recognize those "lines" for what they are. Are you trying to shirk your responsibility as a husband with a cover-up of your professional work? I encourage you to make a plan to cut your travel within the next year. Remember that God is your true Provider. He will honor this effort.

When I started this step of acknowledging Rita's worth, I already had some ideas of the positive differences between my wife and me. In time, I began to see more of her generous spirit with time and money very clearly. Wow!!! It was inspiring. Rita's dad was a good role model for her in being generous. Even though he did not have a lot of money, he knew he was a rich man. His wife and children dearly loved him. He continually showed Rita and me his generosity in many ways.

Rita brought this generous spirit into our marriage. She is very generous with our children in her love, time, and finances. When our two older boys were in high school and our youngest was in third grade, she went back to work part-time. Later, when our youngest son went into junior high, she worked full-time and later became manager of her store. The money she earned in the beginning was primarily used to decorate our home. She made all the rooms come alive with great window and bed treatments. Soon, our entire home had her touch.

As our sons moved out, Rita wanted to make sure their apartments looked and felt like a special place. She saved her money and would surprise them with sofas and decorative accessories for their places. She continues to show her spirit of giving — always of the best. Because I concentrate on telling Rita of her value, I try to acknowledge her generosity more often. I find my love for her unique qualities and gifts increasing as I learn more about her.

Another area that soon became very obvious to me as I "relearned" about my wife is her love and commitment to family. In all honesty, it was far stronger than mine in our early years of marriage. I remember during one of our stormy times when things didn't seem to be working, I didn't feel that my needs were being met and Rita certainly wasn't feeling or being loved. She recommended that we get some counseling to work things out. The work we put into our relationship at that time was worth any cost. Her deep love for family would do anything to keep it on track. I wish I could say that things quickly turned around, but it took a long time to see improvement. Intimacy in our relationship especially increased when I started to use *The Ten* consistently.

The great thing about in-depth learning of a subject is that your desire to learn increases. I have learned a little more about Rita and I'm still interested in learning more. The more I learn, the more I want to know. Believe me, if I can do this step, so can you.

Start first by your own observations of her. Ask the Lord to guide your observations and perceptions of her. He knows your wife better than anyone else — even better than she knows herself — and He can teach you. Notice where she places her efforts and this will tell you where her heart is. Then ask your family members to give you insight into her likes and dislikes. Just be willing to listen to others' opinions and insights of your wife and you will learn.

Let me finish this chapter for those of you who might not feel very loved and are questioning whether this kind of investment and energy is worth it. I would suggest this prayer. Ask our Lord to help you to be willing to go on. Ask Him to create in you the desire to finish well. I will say it over and over throughout this book — with God, all things are possible. Just join with Him and yield to His direction.

Study Questions:
Chapter 4 — Acknowledge her Worth: Say it

1. What do you value in yourself?

2. What are some areas where you struggle with self-worth?

3. List some Scripture verses that would support what God thinks about you.

4. Do you think you have experienced the full impact of what Jesus did on the cross for you? If not, what could help you to internalize it better?

5. List some positive differences between you and your wife. How do these differences help you as a team to meet the challenges of life?

6. How valued was your wife in the family she grew up in? How did her family express value to each other?

7. In what ways can you value her? Share at least two ways.

8. List some ways you could be a student of your wife and family.

9. How can you be a better guardian of your family? What does that mean to you?

Chapter 5 — Laugh and Enjoy Her More
(Days 5, 15, 25)

Is it possible — with all the difficulties of life and the many negative circumstances in this world — that you can honestly find time for real joy and laughter? I personally believe that you can, and that joy and laughter are essential to live a full, well-rounded life. I base my belief on the example we have in the life of Jesus. What could be more serious than redeeming mankind from the wages of sin? His mission was and will always be the greatest event in human history. Yet in spite of this weighty mission, He took time to enjoy His life at every level.

Have you ever heard a statement or concept that you just couldn't relate to at that time? Unfortunately for me, there have been more than I would like to admit. The first time I could remember such an incident I was thirty-one. It was when my life was starting to take a new direction. My old ways weren't working and I was just taking small steps in the beginning of my spiritual journey that would lead me to Jesus. One morning at work, the president of our company stopped in my office to see me (this was an unusual occurrence). After some small talk he said, "Try not to take yourself too seriously." When he walked out I thought, "Is he kidding?" From my perspective, my life was very serious and I needed to figure out some important things. Now, many years later, I aim not to take as many things so seri-

59

ously — business, broken possessions, or a host of other life bumps in the road — because of Jesus' example.

The joy with which Jesus experienced life produced great joy for others. He tells us, "I have told you this so that my joy may be in you and that your joy may be complete." (John 15:11) I can only imagine that Jesus' face beamed when he healed the lame man and saw him jump for joy. When he saw Zaccheus up in a tree, Jesus probably laughed before He called him down and invited Himself over for dinner. Scriptures tell us, "The joy of the Lord is your strength." (Nehemiah 8:11) This shows us that our God is full of joy. You are strong when you are filled with God's joy and you enjoy life and the wife He has given you.

My friend, David and I are in a men's fellowship group together and he is an excellent teacher. He's the kind of guy who teaches others just by sharing his life. One time he told us, "You have to get heavy before you can get light." We all have to get lighter to be able to enjoy life. Many of us fear to take the first step of looking inside ourselves. I have heard many reasons why looking into one's life was to be avoided at all costs. Socrates said, "The unexamined life is not worth living." Being unwilling to do some self-examination, a personal inventory, look into the mirror, or whatever you want to call it, will make it impossible for you to move forward.

For me, the principles in the twelve-step program helped me to really get heavy so I could lighten up. I recommend taking a good look at that type of program, which can be very helpful in breaking bad habits. There are many available, and the tools they provide are invaluable. Jesus said, "First take the plank out of your own eye, and then you will see clearly to remove the speck from your brother's eye." (Matthew 7:5) Jesus was confirming the need for us to work on our own faults before finding fault with someone else.

For most of my life I would not share the real issues with which I was struggling. You can call it a lack of trust or just shame, but I only spoke about what I felt safe sharing. As I write this I've been a believer for more than twenty-eight years, but it has only been in the last four years that I allowed myself to open up to a select few and fully experience God's love and acceptance. Throughout Scripture we are told to have God search our hearts, purify our motives, and clean us of all unrighteousness. This does not happen in a vacuum, so I would encourage you to open up to another man in your life. You need to be a willing participant to put in the hard work — then the results will be God's.

You might ask yourself the following questions to help the process. What are you protecting? What are your fears? What are the unhealthy dependencies you are still bound to? The dependencies that we think are giving us relief and comfort are really just prolonging our pain. You might have some serious character flaws like perfectionism, the need to control, sarcasm, the need to always be right, or the inability to forgive or admit when you are wrong (just to name a few). Give it some thought and you will find areas you don't have the power to fix. You can surrender these to God so you can be healed of these unhealthy attitudes.

You might have some fear of change or of surrendering your life to God's will. Fear of any kind has the potential to become an obsession. Have you ever had success in eliminating fear with willpower alone? My personal experience has not shown me success even though there have been times, in spite of my fears that I still did what I had to do. Wouldn't it be fantastic to have the emotion of fear melt away? It is possible. The victory comes when we accept the fact that *we* can't eliminate it on our own, but *God* can. Jesus says, "This is to my Father's glory, that you bear much fruit, showing yourselves to be my disciples." (John 15:8) His glory comes from doing the work in us and through us. Confront these issues and with God's help, face them with courage. You will find yourself free from their burden and feeling lighter each day.

When it comes to my relationship with my wife, I don't have to take our disagreements so seriously. As a matter of fact, it's getting easier for me to laugh at myself when I mess up. Women appreciate when men are honest with themselves, especially when they admit when they are wrong. I find that it's becoming easier for me to admit and I can actually enjoy not having to always be right.

By lightening up and taking your life not so seriously, your wife will enjoy being around you more. In the fall of 2005, Rita and I took a nice vacation to Italy. It was everything we dreamed it would be. On one of the bus tours, she pointed out a certain building and was able to name it. I disagreed with her about it because I thought it was something else. A little later, she showed me in a book that she was correct. At the time I said, "Rita, you were absolutely right." A woman who was traveling with our group heard me. She said that a man telling his wife that she was right was music to her ears. I must admit that I do have a little fun when I can say it and mean it. So next time your wife is right, don't try to avoid the obvious. Tell her and see her reaction.

My friend David introduced me to another concept I will always use. At one of our meetings, we were talking about fear and what triggers it. David explained a concept that he had labeled a *charge*. Words that are said in anger or harshness carry a big charge, which will always escalate a situation. Gentle words carry a lesser charge and don't cause emotional harm to you or others. David told us that he was always looking for ways to take the charge out of things. This concept really resonated with me.

Over many years of my life, when circumstances were changing or challenging, I realize now that I added a bigger charge to it. After hearing about this concept, I searched for answers as to why I did that. For some reason I felt threatened, especially with failure, and the charge I gave to situations was always bigger than they deserved. With this reaction, it's no wonder I didn't experience more joy and enjoyment with the people around me.

I'm a huge fan of Gary Smalley and John Trent's book, *The Blessing*. It was my foundation for my part of raising our three sons. The third chapter called, *Expressing High Value*, has a section about word pictures that has helped me verbalize some real needs in a way that removes the charge from the situation. This method is just a tool; it's not the only tool. It's like the carpenter who sees all jobs fixable with a hammer. You need more tools, and it will get old if over used.

In the Old Testament, there is a great example of a word picture between friends. Nathan used a word picture to explain to David the wrong he committed with Bathsheba and her husband, Uriah.

"There were two men in a certain town, one rich and the other poor. The rich man had a very large number of sheep and cattle, but the poor man had nothing except one little ewe lamb he had bought. He raised it, and it grew up with him and his children. It shared his food, drank from his cup and even slept in his arms. It was like a daughter to him.

Now a traveler came to the rich man, but the rich man refrained from taking one of his own sheep or cattle to prepare a meal for the traveler who had come to him. Instead, he took the ewe lamb that belonged to the poor man and prepared it for the one who had come to him.

David burned with anger against the man and said to Nathan, "As surely as the Lord lives, the man who did this deserves to die! He must pay for that lamb four times over, because he did such a thing and had no pity."

> Then Nathan said to David, "You are the man!"
> (2 Samuel 12:1-5)

Another way to reduce the negative charge in a situation is to be kinder to yourself. In one of my men's groups, we read from a daily devotional each time we meet. The topic for one day was about making mistakes. The devotion pointed out that just because you make mistakes, you're not the mistake. That sounds so simple but in reality I've often felt when I messed up, I was the mistake. I have learned to be gentler on myself. Being gentler to oneself takes time. Even if you have to put a note on your mirror, "Be kind to yourself," do it. When you start being kind and easier on yourself, you will be kinder to others. It just works that way. So start to be a friend to yourself and soon you will be a friend to your wife.

If I could have changed one thing earlier in our marriage, I wish I could go back and take life easier and enjoy it more. Now that I'm in my sixties, I can see that most of the crises and drama in my personal life and business deals didn't have a lasting effect. Their power was limited to the moment. We have to take responsibility for our part in enjoying any situation — crisis or not.

To deal with a crisis, we need vision that focuses beyond the moment. In Gary Smalley's video series, *Hidden Keys to Loving Relationships*, he reveals a great concept of bonding when things go wrong. The story he told in the video was about camping when a rainstorm flooded their tent. Later, this crisis became a great story evoking lots of laughs every time they retold it. The key is to have a future vision in that tense moment. Know that this too will pass and if you respond well, looking back can bring much laughter.

Here's a classic example for our family of a tense moment when future vision relieved some of the panic. Our whole family packed into the car to drive our first son, Jared, off to

Duquesne University in Pittsburgh. We had an almost new 1985 Town & Country Wagon with his luggage packed on the roof and covered with plastic bags in case of a storm. While driving through the Pennsylvania countryside we started to notice a strong offensive odor. I ventured a guess that it was the smell of the farmers fertilizing their fields. No one challenged me; it sounded reasonable.

As we continued to travel for the next ten minutes, a mist started to cover the windshield and the smell got stronger. I just put on my wipers and began to clear the window. We were the only car on the highway, but soon approached a big truck that had a mist of something shooting out behind it. As we drove toward the truck, we saw that it had a large leak and was spraying everything with this substance. When we were close enough to overtake it on the left, we could read the words, "raw sewage." Everybody screamed, "NO!!!" I pulled over and got out. Our car was covered with this sticky, awful smelling stuff. Jared now felt like he was riding with the Griswalds and couldn't imagine driving on campus and unloading a car covered with raw sewage and smelling like a pig farm.

At the next exit, I pulled off the highway and found a restaurant. I helped my family get settled inside and asked the chef if I could use their water hose in the back. I told him the story and after a good laugh about it, he granted me the water. After I washed off the car and Jared's luggage, the flies that had swarmed around everything finally left and the car was almost back to normal.

That incident brings lots of laughter and shock to those hearing it for the first time. The key is to remember this when you're in a difficult situation: it will be a lot funnier in the future. That will make the moment a lot less tense for everyone involved.

Humor and laughter are great medicines for the soul. "A happy heart makes the face cheerful," (Proverbs 15:13) "A cheerful heart is good medicine," (Proverbs 17:22) Laughter, even in tense moments, can change our attitude of having no hope to seeing the hope in most situations.

When God created us, He created our emotions as part of us. Over the years, I've found myself in many men's groups while different men were dealing with serious issues of very difficult challenges. Sometimes when guys find themselves in a very dark place, another man tells a story about himself that's very funny and we all laugh — even the guy who at that time is carrying a heavy load. I've seen that laughter can help things come back into focus and all is not so dark. Laughter brings the light back.

Being able to laugh at yourself is a good start to adding more joy into your life with your loved ones. However, I feel like I should discuss the flip side to finding humor in everything in life. I've noticed that when I'm in an awkward situation, I rely on my ability to see the humor in the situation. Even though this relieves the awkwardness sometimes, it has the potential to communicate that you're minimizing something very important to your wife or loved one. One of my goals for myself is to work at holding back my humor until the appropriate time. I have learned from my mistakes not to minimize someone else's pain. If you have done that in the past, it's a good time to amend that behavior. It might take some time, but it's worth the work to get it right.

Rita and our youngest son, Peter, share a very special bond. Peter has a great gift of expressing love with hugs and kind words. During his high school years, their friendship and relationship grew even closer as he worked in Rita's store with her. So when the time came for us to drive him to college, it was hard for us, but especially Rita. The exciting part for him was that his two older brothers had their own music business in Nashville, which was very close to his school, so he would still have family close to him. About an hour after we dropped Peter off at Middle Tennessee State

University, I noticed that Rita was crying. I thought for a moment and said, "Are you crying because you're going to miss Peter or because you're going to be all alone with me?" Her tears turned to laughter as she started to smile and laugh, when she realized it was going to be all right.

Laughing and enjoying your wife more is a key to joy and showing appreciation of her in many situations.

Study Questions:
Chapter 5 – Laugh and Enjoy
Her More

1. Can you remember any times when you were growing up how your mother and father enjoyed each other? What did they laugh about?

2. Can you remember when you were dating your wife what you did together and enjoyed?

3. What gets in the way of you enjoying your life and wife more? What Bible verses can you think of that address your concern?

4. What are some practical ways you can enjoy your wife more?

5. When worry or anxiety enters your mind, what are the ways you handle it? What are the results?

6. Make a list of at least five things you can do to enjoy your wife more. Make a plan to put them into action.

7. Is there anything you resent as you go through these steps?

Chapter 6 — Accept Her as She Is: Don't try to Change Her
(Days 6, 16, 26)

Early in our marriage, my wife Rita lightheartedly confronted me every so often of my agenda to make her just like me. Forty-one years later, I'm so glad I wasn't successful. In one of these moments, she told me that if she were just like me, one of us wouldn't be needed. Boy, was she right!

When our pastor, Joel, came to our church, he preached a sermon on celebrating the differences between men and women. The first time I heard him say that I thought, "He's got to be kidding." However, the more I meditated on this simple phrase, it started to sink in. This chapter is going to take a little more effort. Just accepting your wife isn't enough, but we have to celebrate our differences. Of course I am extremely grateful for some of Rita's differences, like our physical differences and her attractiveness. But I wasn't sure I could celebrate our differences until recently. Now I admire her attention to detail, her desire for our home to look good and be comfortable, her financial generosity, and most of all her ability to listen, just to mention a few. We are very different in so many ways and today I can honestly say that I'm grateful it's that way.

I vividly remember the first time I felt truly accepted for who I was. It was in the mid-1980s and I was at a coed twelve-step topic meeting in New York City called, "How have you taken advantage of people?" I had become a Christian in 1977 when I was thirty-two, so I had a broken past that reflected a lost soul. When my turn came, I shared very honestly (probably because the meeting was in New York City — sixty miles from my home) how I had really used people socially, at work, and even used my wife. As I spoke I heard this little voice inside my head saying, "No, you can't share that." At the end of the meeting, many came up to me and gave me hugs and many affirmative words because what came through for the group was my deep sorrow and truly repentant attitude.

The best moment happened about thirty minutes after the meeting ended. As I left this church on Park Avenue, I stopped at the street corner and looked at the church. Then I heard this quiet voice in my mind, "If they accept you, don't you think I do?" That was a powerful moment for me that I will always remember.

As I'm writing this book, I can say that there are times that I don't feel totally accepted by God. When that happens what I remind myself is the fact that Jesus died for me and my sins, then I accept the grace of what He did. It's not my feelings or emotions on which I base my standing; it's the reality and truth of God's word. Because of Jesus, I am fully acceptable to the Father. It took two readings of *The Search for Significance*, by Robert S. McGee for me to see that sometimes we make simple things more complex than they have to be. I recommend that you read this wonderful book as your next book. For me it made what He did on the cross come alive in me again. I saw how easy it is for us to believe the lie that we are not acceptable.

I understand now that if I wasn't able to accept this foundational truth, I really was not experiencing the totality of the Christian life. While I was reading *The Search for Significance,* it became clear that I did not really understand my identity of who I am in Christ. Then I held a men's study on this topic, and it became very clear that many men struggle with the same problem. After accepting Jesus as Savior and Lord are we really acceptable and pleasing to the Father? Even though this is hard for us to believe, the answer is a resounding, "Yes." God the Father said that the work of Jesus on the cross was perfect; the steps needed for reconciliation to our Father were complete. The more I read that, the more it took on greater meaning. Because of Jesus, God accepted me and I am no longer condemned.

I want to spend a little more time discussing how we receive our acceptance before I get back to how we can become more accepting of our wives. I think there is a major connection between how we accept or reject ourselves and how we accept or reject others.

All of us were at one time (or still are) held in captivity by the weight of wrath on our lives. When we accept the sacrifice Jesus made on our behalf, the Father says, "Welcome into my kingdom. You see your actions or work had nothing to do with it. It was when you accepted Him. He covers you with his righteousness." (Read John 3:16 with fresh eyes and notice that this is what it says). Isn't it strange that the acceptance we were freely given, we don't freely give? This is why I believe that accepting others is directly related to accepting God's forgiveness for our sins and accepting ourselves just the way we are. Only then can we accept others as they are.

How does this happen? It's simple, but not easy. Everybody knows that if you want to lose weight, you should eat less and exercise. That's simple. But we know it's not easy. Just think of the number of books, programs, and pills that are sold to help us do this simple thing. In this same way, acceptance is simple but it's not easy. Jesus gave us a great clue when He said, "First take the plank out of your own eye, and then you will see clearly to remove the speck from your brother's eye." (Matthew 7:5) What did Jesus know about you and me? Probably that it was easier for us to point out the problems of others and tell them how to solve them, than it is to deal with our own difficulties. I guess this is just part of our old nature. We tend to judge others before we even consider what's wrong with ourselves.

When I first heard the following, I didn't believe it. The only person you can change is yourself. This is similar to the old saying, "You can lead a horse to water, but you can't make him drink." Well, let's throw some salt into his mouth to make him thirsty! Then he'll change. So how do we "throw salt" into someone's mouth? I think it's by being the person God wants you to be. Show His love and carry an attitude of respect. This will be the best teacher for those around you. As St. Francis of Assisi said, "Preach the Gospel at all times, use words if necessary."

I can only imagine being around Jesus as He demonstrated His nature to those who were following Him. I don't picture a lot of finger pointing or negative put downs, but I see His grace and kindness displayed to those around Him. When we show love, grace, kindness, and patience to those around us, we can be an encouragement to those around us to act differently.

I'm sure you are thinking, "What about the Pharisees or priests? Jesus didn't refrain from calling them some pretty strong names." Yes, He exposed them because they were covering up their deceit, pride, and phoniness. Before we ever feel we can expose someone like this, we need to deal with our own dishonesty, egotism, and hypocrisy. Once we see who we are, we should confess it to Jesus and He will help restore us. Remember when Jesus said to them, "Your eye is a lamp for your body. A pure eye lets sunshine into your soul. But an evil eye shuts out the light and plunges you into darkness. Make sure that the light you think you have is not really darkness." (Luke 11:34-35) All Jesus wants from us is our heartfelt desire to seek His help in healing our bad attitudes and resentment. It all starts with seeing and accepting the character flaws in ourselves. Only then can healing start to take place.

When I learned this vital lesson of others accepting me just as I am, it was life changing. Unfortunately it's a life long process. To maintain acceptance of others takes continual self-searching honesty and openness with close friends. When I'm not in a men's fellowship group or a good accountability relationship with another guy, I can get to the place where I think I'm pretty special and have no problems, and just offer my solutions for everyone else.

If the pain we are experiencing still allows us to function, we think we're okay. I find it amazing how much resentment, anger, and pain men can endure. We finally acknowledge it when it surfaces in some physical way like tension, ulcers, or back or head aches. Most guys think they can do it alone, but this is a lie we can never afford to buy into because isolation ultimately spells death. Initially it was my pain that led me into twelve-step work and to connect to a good men's group in our church. What keeps me connected is easy; I see the positive results in me. I become more accepting of others, less opinionated, and more open and honest with myself. The greatest improvement is that my relationship with my wife and family keeps improving. Why would I stop? Why are you waiting to try it?

Many years ago while driving to New Jersey, I was listening to a Christian radio station and the host said, "Acceptance produces change." I knew that concept was alive in my life. I thought about the way God accepts me exactly the way I am and that He was producing changes in me in a very quiet and gentle way. I formerly confused acceptance with apathy. Acceptance is this: You see a situation for what it is. Then with no excuses or denials, you are able to admit that you have a problem. Apathy is totally different. Apathy is this: You see your situation as hopeless, believe that you can't change and that there is nothing you could do to make it better. Acceptance actually frees us. When we acknowledge a problem, we can accept it and ask God for help to change.

The first time I saw the power of acceptance in our marriage goes back a while but the truth I learned from the experience lives on.

I became a Christian in September of 1977. The personal changes were very obvious to those who knew me. To say it bluntly, I became a zealot for Jesus and Rita became my most important mission. As I write this, I remember what a jerk I was to her back then. Since I am a driven salesman, I used similar tactics in sharing my newfound faith and I was relentless. I would leave tracts around the house and could turn any given conversation into a spiritual conversation. During the first six months, Rita was bombarded with the gospel. She already knew the story and the more I spoke of it, I saw that her spirit was closing down.

About eight months into this persistent method, I was given some great advice at a prayer meeting. I was lamenting about my wife's unbelief and feeling very sorry for myself when a kinder, older, and much wiser person shared a great lesson. He placed three cups in a row on a table. Pointing at the first cup he said, "This is Rita." Then pointing at the cup farthest away he said, "This is Jesus." Pointing at the middle cup he said, "And this is you. You're blocking her view. Get out of the way so she can see Jesus." When I heard that message, I knew it was true — I was the problem.

So I got out of the way. I stopped preaching and started to accept her unconditionally. The first thing that I noticed was that the tension between us was gone. I started to live my life without trying to make her a Christian because I now understood that she would have to come to Jesus on her own in the same way I did.

If I close my eyes, I can still see it. Early one morning in December 1978, I walked into our kitchen. Rita was still in her robe and she turned to me and said, "I want to let you know that I've made your Jesus my Jesus." I hugged her so hard and the tears came. I knew in my heart that now we could make it. With two of us in Him we could meet whatever lay ahead.

Rita later explained what had happened and it was very encouraging. She told me that one night while looking at the stars, she asked God to restore her marriage and to show her who He was. It happened in an instant. He communicated to her that He was God and it all became clear. But I know that this was only possible because I got out of the way and stopped trying to change her.

Another part of acceptance is to learn to let go of the results — that is God's part. I think the *Serenity Prayer* is extremely useful. "God grant me the serenity to accept the things I cannot change; courage to change the things I can; and wisdom to know the difference." It takes courage to do *The Ten*, but letting go of the results is even more difficult.

Remember that this isn't going to happen overnight; this is a lifelong process. It's easier than you think it is to slip back into bad behavior. It reminds me of this proverb, "As a dog returns to its vomit, so a fool repeats his folly." (Proverbs 26:11) I think acknowledging this about ourselves is vital to any real change. The former alcoholic knows it well. After ten, twenty, or even thirty years of sobriety, he is still one drink away from being a drunk again. When we understand that we need to be vigilant in our own personal recovery and growth, we can become the man God knows we can be.

Let me tell you another interesting story. I tend to be a promoter, which is a nice way of saying, "I have something good for you to do and you should do it." My wife has become aware of these "promotions" of mine and she sees them as an attempt to manipulate her. Needless to say after forty-one years of marriage, she senses this manipulation very quickly. In November 2000, I started to workout on a regular basis at least three times a week. Naturally I felt better and started to even look better. At first I would say, "Come on, Rita. Join me at the club. We can workout together. You'll love it."

My real reason for wanting her to come with me wasn't because I thought she'd like it; I was being totally selfish. My wife and I had gained some extra weight over the years. I wanted her to come to the gym to workout with me and get that body of hers back to what I remembered it was when she was thirty. Now, I have to tell you that I wasn't subtle — I promoted the positive health aspects, but deep down I wanted the body she had when she was younger. Yes, I'm shallow that way but I have gotten better once I started working this step. For about three years, I would gently remind her by talking about our later years together or about the studies that show that exercise adds up to living a stronger and healthier life. Nothing worked. Finally I just accepted that and acknowledged that my real motives for wanting her to workout were not for her benefit, but for mine.

Then I started to follow this simple plan: I just went to the gym for myself and continued to love her just the way she was. I loved her with no conditions, no expectations, just acceptance. A couple of great things happened. Once my mind was off this desire, I was able to move on and just enjoy her exactly the way she was. The next change really surprised me. One night she came home and told me that she had signed up at a fitness place for women. Since then, she has been going faithfully. What's really great is that I'm happy for her because I know it's good for her. I would be dishonest with you if I said I wasn't pleased for myself, but I am. My wife is a great looking woman. That's what attracted me to her over forty years ago. She has a lot more than looks in her favor today, but I'll not be disappointed if her body starts to show the efforts of her work.

After all this time and many failed attempts, I know that I cannot change Rita. One thing I have learned is that acceptance does produce change. I now have the courage to change the things I can, which became *The Ten*. And this method has worked for me. *My* changes have brought about a much better relationship between us. Men, when we let go of our compulsive, controlling, and demanding ways, changes happen. The first major difference I noticed when I stopped trying to change Rita was that she started to trust me more. And with this newfound trust came more intimacy and enjoyment. All these examples are to show you that I have learned first-hand that acceptance does work.

I would like to end with some additional thoughts for those of you who might have wives who really need to be confronted of behavior that's destructive to them and others. I'm talking about addictions, unfaithfulness, stealing, cheating, or even physical abuse. Acceptance is still needed, but it looks different. You might be in denial, tend to make excuses for her behavior, or even blame yourself for what she is doing. Well, when you come to accept that she is _____ (you can fill in the blank), intervention is needed. I would encourage you to first get counseling for yourself; get the best advice you can from the best. Pray constantly for God's guidance, strength, and pray the *Serenity Prayer*. When you have prayed, sought counsel, and received other trusted men's input, then it's time to confront your wife. You will need a good support group as you move through these tough steps. But once you have stopped making excuses and accept what your situation is, you will need support.

Depending how on much denial your wife is in, when you act in a compassionate and loving way using tools from a counselor, she will be forced to face her destructive behavior. You can't force her to change, but your change will have a positive effect on her.

Remember that it is God's goodness that leads us to repentance and sometimes His goodness is seen through tough love in our lives. Keep working this program and stay focused on making these changes in your life. You will see that those around you will find you more attractive in the same way that people found Jesus attractive and wanted to be around Him.

Let me end this chapter with the following observation. I really dislike it when I sense that people are trying to "fix" me. It sends all sorts of bad signals: I'm being rejected, I'm inadequate the way I am, and mostly I sense a lack of respect of who I am. Think about how your wife must feel when you send her these kinds of messages by trying to get her to change. What you are really communicating is that she's missing the mark and you're demonstrating a very conditional love. Don't ask her to change, but let it go. Work these steps one day at a time. Ask God for the power to carry them out and leave the results to Him.

Study Questions:
Chapter 6 — Accept Her as She Is
— Don't Try to Change Her

1. We know that Scripture tells us that God accepts us just the way we are. Have you experienced that yet?

2. What have been some things about yourself that you struggle with and still can't accept about yourself? What about your wife?

3. Have you ever gone through a time you wished your wife was different? Explain the specifics.

4. How have you in the past and present communicated with your wife her shortcomings or changes you wanted her to make? What worked? What didn't work?

5. What is an area that you need to work on with accepting your wife? What makes this difficult?

6. Can you list at least five aspects of your wife's personality that you appreciate?

7. Why do you think by pointing out someone's shortcomings that it will remedy the situation? What is the best way you have found to discuss areas that really need change, such as poor life-style, health choices, etc?

Chapter 7 – Show Her Compassion
(Days 7, 17, 27)

Like most of the other steps in this book, showing compassion to your wife and family must start with learning to show compassion to yourself. It is impossible to give something you don't have. The problem is that you probably don't know how to acquire compassion or even have a clear idea of what being compassionate means.

How many men confuse the word compassion with being weak? If you have seen the movie *Patton* with George C. Scott portraying General Patton, you would remember the scene when the traumatized soldier was telling General Patton that he was afraid. Patton responded with anger, slapped him, and treated him like he was a coward. I remember thinking, "What was wrong with him that he had to react with such anger? What was it that prohibited him from showing compassion? Is it true that compassion equals weakness and weakness is a disgrace?" After some time of reflection, I know that these things are not true. Compassion is not a weakness, but a strength.

Learning to be more kind to ourselves is not easy for most of us. When we were growing up, we learned that boys do not show emotion because being tender is not what men do. One current way I've seen a change in that old model is in the pictures of our soldiers in Iraq. Many of these pictures show our warriors holding children or praying with each other. They are very moving and reveal a great deal of the heart of a man.

Over the years, I've had some wonderful relationships mentoring young men. It's always difficult to see men struggle with their personal value. How much of their value is tied to their success? This is something with which I am familiar. I believe God has made men "doing beings" with purpose and drive, and that accomplishments are inherently important to us. The problem comes when we only measure ourselves by our external accomplishments. It's sad to say that when we aren't good at or even fail at a job, we think we are failures. Instead of telling ourselves, "I've made a mistake," we think, "I must be the mistake."

I met one young man when he was in the middle of an emotional meltdown during college. This was the beginning of a long time friendship because both of us are very similar even though I am many years older. The greatest similarity that we share is that we can show great patience and care to others, but cannot be gentle, forgiving, and kind to ourselves. When we met, I knew that the standard he had set for himself was so high that any small miss of the mark triggered waves of anxiety about failure within. Being threatened by failure is not uncommon for men. Some men just cover it up well — from being a workaholic to struggling with a number of other addictions.

I had an experience of confusing my work and my own value in October 2000. At work, I noticed that orders for my business were slowing down — almost stopping. I finished that year well, won an award trip and made good incentive, however it was the first time in seventeen years that I was going into a new year without any business in the works or deals close to being orders. In January 2001, I did what every hard working, compulsive salesman does — I prayed harder and worked harder. I realize now that my prayers were more about asking for opportunities and business than asking the Lord to show me what I needed to learn. That came much later.

In February 2001, my active pace led to very active anxiety. I could not believe what my mind was telling me. When I got the first sales sheet in my life that showed a month with $0 sales, I went into an emotional tailspin. My mind was telling me loud and clear that I was a "ZERO."

The mind can be a wonderful thing, but it can also be our worst enemy when it turns on us. We are not the only one who puts thoughts into our minds. There's a story in Matthew when Jesus asked Peter, "'Who do you say I am?' Simon Peter answered, 'You are the Christ, the Son of the living God.' Jesus replied, 'Blessed are you, Simon, son of Jonah, for this was not revealed to you by man, but by my Father in heaven.'" (Matthew 16:15-17) God puts good, healthy thoughts in our minds. He speaks to us in truth.

In the very next story, Jesus tells his disciples he was going to the cross. "Peter took him aside and began to rebuke him. 'Never, Lord!' he said, 'This shall never happen to you!' Jesus turned and said to Peter, 'Get behind me, Satan!'" (Matthew 16: 22-23) Jesus knew that Peter was speaking words that hadn't come from His Father in heaven but from the father of lies, Satan. Peter's example shows us that Satan had a way of gaining access into his thoughts. Satan still has the power to put thoughts into our minds. I believe that when I saw my business start to dry up, Satan added to my negative feelings with his tormenting ideas. After I became a Christian, there is no other time I can remember such an onslaught of hurtful and discouraging thoughts flooding my mind over a two-week period. Satan was relentless with me at that time.

The remedy I sought was prayer. I went to the elders at our church and shared my condition and pain. I received love, acceptance, encouragement, hope, and fellowship. I went back to a twelve-step group to have a safe place to share and to start my surrendering process again. Confession was also important to this remedy. I sought out a friend whom I trusted to be my sponsor and accountability partner. This process of prayer and confession worked. For the next year, I committed myself to move into a new phase of my life. I put in the effort at work and accepted the results. God's truth is that we can plant, we can water, but the growth is God's — even at work. When the Holy Spirit makes God's truth come alive in us, something exciting happens: fear and confusion are replaced by peace and serenity. I now believe that truth and embrace it.

I wish I could tell you that my journey was a short one, but it wasn't. After three and a half years of the poorest sales I had ever had, I saw where God's growth was happening: in me, but not my business. With the help of some good friends, reading Scripture every day, and working through studies like *The Search for Significance*, I came out with less of the old John and more of the new. That three and a half year experience helped me see that it was always Him. I formerly thought that *I* was the agent of success and change. I discovered that it was always *Him*; I was only the vessel.

My three and a half years of lean times ended in August of 2004. One morning I was reading in the book of James. It said, "Elijah was a man just like us. He prayed earnestly that it would not rain, and it did not rain on the land for three and a half years. Again he prayed, and the heavens gave rain, and the earth produced its crops." (James 5:17-18) I counted from February 2001 — when I hit bottom — until that morning. It was exactly three and a half years. I read Scripture every morning, but that morning the verse jumped out at me as if I was being told that my lean time had ended.

The difference in me after these three and a half years was that my peace and confidence was now in God. My emotional well-being was not based on going from one business success to another, but on His promise and provision.

God helped me to keep my focus on Him. By mid-August, I booked more business than I did in the entire year of 2003 — and it continued. I ended that year 300% higher than the previous year and also earned a sales award trip, which I hadn't done in years. The difference in me now was my fear of failure had been replaced with faith in Him to be a trustworthy, loving God who would not leave, forsake, or humiliate me.

When our Lord is able to help us shed some of our dependencies, we can be truly free to be ourselves. In *The Serenity Bible* (which is a companion for twelve-step recovery programs), the first step says that, "We admitted we were powerless over our addiction – that our lives had become unmanageable." This could mean any addictive agent through which we have sought to meet our deepest needs — money, sex, career, a chemical agent — anything and everything about which we have become excessive must be put in proper perspective. None of these things deserve to be lifted onto a pedestal to be worshipped.

There is only one way I know to release these dependencies and it's through step two. I love their definition of the next step, "Came to believe that a Power greater than ourselves could restore us to sanity." With humility and prayer, ask God to lead and guide you into serenity. Become a willing participant as He shows you the way to restore your life, usually through people He sends into your life.

When you start moving in this direction, it's amazing how much easier it becomes to meet the needs of others. When you start trusting God for the results, and continue to do the footwork — WOW! There is fruit in that. When I first heard, "Let go, let God." I thought, "What a cop-out." But slowly I began to understand it. Like any principle, people can misuse this idea by thinking that they don't need to put in any effort because God will take care of everything. The truth is that only when I have done all I can, I let go and the results are God's. A good example of this idea is putting an effort into these ten steps. The effort is yours, but the results are God's.

Just do *The Ten* one step at a time. Start step seven today with one little saying, "I might fail, but I'm not a failure." You are fearfully and wonderfully made. God created each one of us as a one-of-a-kind. In God's economy, there are no failures because we're all in process.

After thirty-one years of my relationship with our Lord, I can say that some situations that I thought were failures or losses were truly gains. "Trust in the Lord with all your heart and lean not on your own understanding; in all your ways acknowledge him, and he will make your paths straight." (Proverbs 3:5-6) These verses are true — God wants us to trust Him to guide us through both success and failure.

The most challenging time to be compassionate with ourselves is when we have failed. In 1967, I reached the final step in an interviewing process with a medium-sized company. My final meeting was in a restaurant in New York City with the eastern regional sales manager, the man I would ultimately work under. The luncheon started well but turned out badly. He told me that I needed more training to sell in New York City. He also bluntly said that I wasn't as good as I thought I was. I don't ever remember being challenged this directly, so I got mad. I put down my money to pay for my part of the meal and walked out. He followed me to my car and continued arguing with me.

I had been selling since I was twelve-years-old — first door-to-door magazines, then I sold packaging for a small converter on Long Island. By the age of twenty-two, I had a lot of success selling in New York City and I told him so. It got loud and ugly. When I got home that night, I explained to Rita that I really blew it. We both knew that this wasn't the end of the world and I knew I would get to work for the right company.

Only a few days later, I got a call from another man saying that I had really impressed John (the person with whom I had lunch) and that John wanted me to work for him. I was stunned, but I negotiated a good contract. I increased my salary by fifty percent, got great benefits, and most importantly — a future.

I learned the business quickly by going to every training session I could. When I visited our plants, I would absorb all the important information. I had always been a natural closer with high energy and interpersonal skills. Now with more knowledge and a growing company behind me, the sky was the limit.

Within the first year, I was opening accounts. By my second year, I had opened accounts at two of the largest companies in New York City that had a reputation of turning away salesmen in our company. By the third year, my sales had tripled and I received maximum bonuses. During those years, my relationship with John, my boss, was a hard one. He seldom complimented me or personally told me that he thought I was doing well. One time, he gave me an award at a major sales meeting. It was a pewter plate and he didn't have my name engraved on it, nor the reason why I was receiving the award. He told me he didn't want any praise to go to my head. Sometimes others told me of a compliment he gave me, but that was all. He did petition to get me raises, so I never had to ask. I think he took some pride in how well his men did.

Each year it became a greater challenge to beat the prior year. Soon I was promoted to be the youngest sales manager in the company. The group I managed also did well and our territory increased by thirty percent almost every year. During my first ten years there, our division went from $78-million to over $400-million, but this growth did not come without some personal sacrifice. The pressure to keep increasing sales was taking a toll on some of us. If you didn't perform, you were fired. My boss, John was the one who would do all the hiring and firing. I think he enjoyed firing his employees, especially if they had a visible vulnerability. He was not subtle in letting a person know their inadequacies before he fired them.

At the same time, my relationship with him continued to grow tense. I was burning the candle at both ends and had started to see my own character flaws. This realization took me through my own personal crisis. While I was trying to find my new road (which looked like a spiritual one), John was facing his own crisis. As demands increased, he argued with major department heads. He sought out conflict and burned many bridges. His targets were getting bigger and his anger greater. Then it happened: he was fired. I couldn't believe it because I thought no one could take him down; he was too formidable.

John was just in his forties when he was fired. Only a few us truly understood what happened next. One Sunday morning in August 1977, he took his golf clubs and a twelve-gauge shotgun into a park. He placed the barrel in his mouth and pulled the trigger. I got the call when I was at a coworker's home at the Jersey shore. We were stunned — John had committed suicide.

John's young, attractive wife and two children attended the funeral. I was numb with shock and still trying to find my own road. I had given some thought to doing the same thing a year earlier, so I questioned God — why him, why not me? Why was I given a second chance? As the years went by it became clear. John was not a man who could give any compassion or empathy to others. Not only did he have trouble showing compassion to others, but he also couldn't be gentle on himself. Before he died, he weighed himself by his own standards and found himself wanting. The next natural thing he had to do was execute the punishment for this kind of failure — death.

I have some big questions for you. Do you weigh your-self and find yourself wanting? In what areas do you need to show compassion to yourself? How can you begin this change?

The first change you can make is in your internal dialogue. When you're faced with an outcome you disagree with, speak kindly to yourself. A few years ago, I attended a trade show in New York City and I didn't get much out of it. I felt like I had wasted my time and my company's money by attending. As I left the building, my mind was filled with many thoughts that were hard and hurtful. I knew that my heavenly Father wouldn't talk to me that way. I needed to reject those thoughts and I did.

My test for these condemning thoughts in my head is to challenge them with, "Would my Father in heaven speak to me that way?" or, "What does the Bible say to me about this?" When you see that your thoughts are contrary to either of these questions, don't accept the condemnation. Rebuke the thoughts as Satan's lies and replace them with God's truth. You will have to do this many times, but it will pay major dividends. You must take every thought that conflicts with God's word and His love of you captive. By doing this, you are on a great start to becoming more compassionate.

How would your thinking change if you took most of your negative thoughts captive and replaced them with posi-tive thoughts? Scripture tells us, "Finally brothers, whatever is true, whatever is noble, whatever is right, whatever is pure, whatever is lovely, whatever is admirable — if anything is excellent or praiseworthy — think about such things." (Philippians 4:8)

You might say that this is impossible, but I would remind you that we have a wonderful God. Attempting to do this alone will only get us so far; this journey starts with faith. I'm talking about the same faith that David had when he faced Goliath. He trusted that God would go before him and give him victory. By faith, humbly ask God to remove your negative thoughts and replace them with thoughts that are true, noble, and virtuous. It is possible — all things are possible with God. When it comes to restoring our hearts and minds, we have the unending power of the Holy Spirit. Just put in the footwork. The process might take time, but you will see the results.

I have some suggestions to help you get started. If you want to have clean water running through your mind, you need to turn off the muddy water. There's a child's song that says, "Oh, be careful little eyes what you see. Be careful little ears, what you hear." Ask the Holy Spirit to show you what you need to tune out. I had to let go of a variety of TV and radio programs, and now I try to make better movie choices. Stop the flow of the negative and start the new flow.

Here's the next challenge. So how do we incorporate *Step Seven* — showing compassion and becoming a person of compassion into our lives with others? This is a decision just like choosing to love someone: it is a *decision*, not a feeling. I can't remind you of that enough.

Maybe you can learn from my mistakes. I will share two stories about compassion: one where I failed to show compassion and another time when I did better. I want to remind you before these stories that I still struggle with doing *The Ten* all the time. I'm just human. I am still working on this and by God's grace will become more compassionate.

About ten years ago, my wife had surgery on both feet at the same time. I have to admit even though I had been a Christian for some time and I knew better, I was totally out to lunch on this. Our youngest son, Peter, took her to the hospital and brought her back home. I wasn't even around when she got home. Years later, we were talking and this operation came up. She told me how painful the healing was and that my absence before and after the surgery was equally painful. She didn't want to make a big deal about it, but it spoke volumes to me.

Later, I thought about what I do for my customers. I have a motto at work that my job is to serve and protect. I should serve our clients with all of our resources and an attitude of gratitude. Also, I protect them and their company by spotting danger signs and helping them avoid pitfalls. Rita is the most important person in my life to whom I have taken a very serious vow — love, honor, protect, and care for in sickness and health, whether we are rich or poor, until death parts us. I recognize now that at that time, I failed in the "care for" part because my priorities had not been in the correct order. I know there are times when we are faced with the urgency of the moment, especially when we have a demanding job. Usually when I look back, I see that all those pressing problems did get resolved. Then I wonder why I worried about it so much.

When I was learning this step, I tried to envision what I would want someone to do for me in Rita's situation. What could they say or do to help me feel better? Then I would do those things for her. Another approach to this is to think of your best friend and how you would respond to him if he were in pain. Hopefully this will help you to change your response to your family. Each time you need help showing compassion, pray this prayer, "May the words of my mouth and the meditation of my heart be pleasing in your sight, O Lord, my Rock and my Redeemer." (Psalm 19:14)

Remember to respond from your heart, not your head. Most men have a tendency to respond with the head by offering help through solutions. This doesn't leave much room for compassion. Put yourself in your wife's shoes and try to imagine how she is hurting. This will help you get in touch with your heart so you can respond compassionately.

If your words are coming out harsh or hurtful, you are still responding out of fear not faith. You can say a lot to a person as long as there is love in your words. If it's not coming from a place of honest love, wait until it is. Don't say it in that moment.

The time when I was able to demonstrate more compassion was when Rita's parents came to our home for part of the summer. I had known Rita's dad since I was a teenager and now that I was in my fifties, our relationship was very special. Over the years, I had really grown to love him. The quality I admired most about him was his unfailing commitment to family and the way he cared for them.

In preparation of their arrival, I fixed up the small cottage we have on our property. It's a great little place for people to stay when they visit. I spent two months cleaning, sanding, and painting. In the screened-in-porch, I made a workbench for his hobbies. When I had finished, the whole cottage looked great. It was going to be a great summer for them.

The only problem was that his health was deteriorating very quickly. When they arrived in Connecticut, it was apparent to us that he was walking slower and his energy level was lower. Within a few weeks, he was admitted to the hospital and we were told that many of his vital organs were shutting down. It was very clear that he was not going to make it. We immediately called his brothers and all his daughters and their husbands. I did whatever was needed to help get everybody in to see him. For the next ten days, I was "Mister Taxi," going to and from the airport. We managed to have his entire family fly in. They all stayed at our home and that time was very special. My wife took off from work to be with him. We were all around his bed reciting the 23rd Psalm until he took his last breath. This time, I got my priorities right.

During that time I learned many things, but I wouldn't have learned anything if I hadn't been physically there. Being present at Rita's dad's passing moved me. I can still envision it: everyone was holding hands and praying. Those last few days and final moments for him were the most meaningful to my wife and other family members who were there. It is during these times that your heart is open for change. I call them life-defining moments. You can only receive them if you are actually there.

We need to believe God when he said, "Come to me, all who are weary and burdened, and I will give you rest. Take my yoke upon you and learn from me, for I am gentle and humble in heart, and you will find rest for your souls. For my yoke is easy and my burden is light." (Matthew 11:28-30) This is hard to believe or even comprehend, but it is true. His yoke is easy and He is willing to share our burdens. The question is, can we trust Him more than we trust ourselves? I've always admired men who seemed to go through life without as much stress and worry as I have. This gives you the freedom to respond with compassion when it is needed. I now know that it's all about letting go. In order to let go, do the footwork, which is what you know needs to be done. Then leave the results to God. In the last few years, I've learned this lesson well.

Study Questions:
Chapter 7 — Show Her Compassion

1. Do you wrestle with showing compassion because you think it's a sign of weakness?

2. In movies you have seen or books you have read, can you think of a character that shows compassion or refuses to show compassion? What do they do that touches you?

3. When growing up, who do you remember as the most compassionate person in your family? Can you remember receiving compassion when you needed it?

4. When could you have been more compassionate with someone in your family? Is it still an open wound for you or the person who needed you? What would you do differently today?

5. What are some ways to show compassion to your wife that would be meaningful to her?

6. To do: Next time your wife is upset, over worked, or stressed out, look her in the eye and in a compassionate tone say, "What can I do to help?" Then listen carefully to her response, stop what you're doing and help.

Chapter 8 — Enjoy Your Life Together
(Days 8, 18, 28)

To start this step, I have two questions for you. Have you given yourself permission to truly enjoy your life? Do you have the ability to stay in the moment and really take in what's happening around you whether it's good or bad? Jesus teaches us how important it is to live in the moment. One of the most profound things Jesus was able to do was to think of others up to the very moment He was crucified. Could you imagine how paralyzed with fear you or I would be if we knew the fate that lay ahead of us if we were to be whipped and crucified? When you read Matthew 26, Mark 14, or Luke 22, you see Jesus totally focused on others to the very end. He was able to live in the moment. It's something we must learn in order to deepen our relationship with God and others around us.

In twelve-step work, an important part of recovery is to stay in the present without projecting into the future. Have you ever noticed how much of your time is spent five minutes, five hours, or five days ahead or in the past? Just for fun, do a test for yourself. Increase your awareness about how much of your thought life is spent projecting into the future or reviewing the past. If you find that it's more than half of your thoughts, this chapter is especially for you.

Sometimes we don't fully understand the extent of our fallen nature and how this affects our lack of discipline over our minds. This lack of control obstructs the abundant life that Jesus promised us. We know it would be hard to swim in a pool filled with debris. In the same way, it's hard to experience peace and joy when your mind is cluttered.

I have a friend who tells me that he actually believes that his worry keeps bad things from happening. By worrying he even keeps the ceiling from falling down. I call these thoughts "joy robbers" and we must spend some time looking at this before we tackle the "enjoy" part of step eight.

Did you know that most of what people worry about never actually happens? The root of worry is actually fear. There are many types of fear — fear of failure, abandonment, sickness — the list goes on and on. Faith is the absolute opposite of fear, because where there is faith there is no fear. Only in the darkest moments of my life, my faith was replaced by fear. I received Christ Jesus, so I know God does not condemn me. This means that I should not fear God, and for that reason I truly have nothing to fear. Please give this some thought. You are no longer separated, judged, or punished by God and you are totally pleasing and acceptable to God because of the finished work of Jesus. Meditate on this truth, "For God did not send his Son into the world to condemn the world, but to save the world through him... Whoever believes in the Son has eternal life, but whoever rejects the Son will not see life, for God's wrath remains on him." (John 3:17 and 36)

Satan is a thief, deceiver, and destroyer who perverts all that is good. I think that Simon Peter was able to write about Satan with conviction based on his experience. "Simon, Simon, Satan has asked to sift you as wheat. But I have prayed for you, Simon, that your faith may not fail. And when you have turned back, strengthen your brothers." (Luke 22:31-32) Peter later instructs us, "Be self-controlled and alert. Your enemy the devil prowls around like a roaring lion looking for someone to devour. Resist him, standing firm in the faith, because you know that your brothers throughout the world are undergoing the same kind of sufferings. And the God of all grace, who called you to his eternal glory in Christ, after you have suffered a little while, will himself restore you and make you strong, firm, and steadfast." (1 Peter 5:8-10) Most assuredly, Peter wanted us to know that Satan's desire is to rob us of our peace and serenity by exchanging our good moments with doubt, confusion, and worry. Satan is a master of putting thoughts into our minds with an objective to destroy our peace of mind and bring us into despair, helplessness, and hopelessness. We need to address those thoughts when they come into our heads before we can begin to enjoy the present moment.

We were discussing spiritual warfare in a men's group when my co-leader, Stan, reminded us of Greg's story about Satan's strategies. It's so powerful I'm going to share it. Greg told us that he was very good at ping-pong when he was younger. When he played someone new, he quickly learned his or her weaknesses in the game. Once he had determined his opponent's weakness, he played hard to that weakness. His conclusion was that Satan and his tormenters study us in the same way. They search for our weaknesses, and then develop a strategy to defeat us.

The pastor at our church, Clive, recently reminded us that God wants us to succeed. He wants us to do well. When He tests us, He cheers for us to score well, pass the test, and ultimately learn from the experience. Satan wants the exact opposite. He tempts us and wants us to fail, and then he uses this failure against us to condemn us. His strategy is to use our weaknesses to coax us away from God. It can be frightening to think that God allows Satan to tempt us in this way. Let me remind you that our Lord is sovereign. Satan is on a tight leash and nothing can happen to you without it passing through God. One of the most difficult concepts to understand is that sometimes God allows what He hates in order to accomplish what He loves. I know this well because I have learned the most from the darkest and most painful times in my life.

In these dark and painful times, man's tendency is to cut and run when the situation or pain becomes too great. Jesus said in Gethsemane, "The spirit is willing, but the body is weak." (Matthew 26:41) Make no doubt about it, you are weak on your own, but God is willing to change you through His Holy Spirit. When I look back over the years, the times I felt the most value and worth were in those moments when all hell was breaking on me but I didn't run. I leaned completely on Jesus to see me through and He was faithful to me each time. He is willing and able to carry you through any situation you encounter in life.

My opinion based on experience, is that our fallen nature and emotions are easy targets for Satan's attacks. If we tend to be negative, have self-pity, or blame others, he will feed on that. We need to recognize these attacks for what they are and develop a strategy against him. Let me suggest the following. First, understand that the stakes are high. If you knew there was a predator in your home with a desire to kill your family, you would take all the right actions to eliminate that threat. Recognize these negative thoughts or feelings as if there were a predator in your mind. Prayer is the most powerful weapon God gives us for this battle. Start praying early in the morning and don't finish your prayer for that day until you lay your head down at night. Pray specifically for your family's safety because praying for your family is one of the most important things you can do for them. Pray that God will increase your knowledge of Him so you can experience His fullness and love. Ask Him for the humility to yield to His will, the courage to change, and the power to carry out what He asks of you.

We all know what our personal weaknesses are. We know what catches our attention and the direction our thoughts tend to go. This is one of the best reasons to stay connected to a good men's group. You can talk freely about your weakness with someone who shares that same weakness. He might have good insight about ways you can combat this weakness. A good way to locate this special brother is to ask God to put a person into your life who could help you to grow. He will answer your prayer; you just need to be open. Remember that God's choice for you might not be the same man you would have chosen for yourself. I found it usually works that way, but also that it works best when I follow God's guidance.

These weaknesses turn into battles when we are determined not to give in to them. We face many battles in this life — some are physical, like fatigue or sickness — but the major battles are in the mind. Several months ago, my mentor gave me the following verse. "I made a covenant with my eyes not to look lustfully at a girl." (Job 31:1) If God said that there was no one like Job on earth and we can read that Job had to guard his eyes and what he might think about, I realized that this was a vital part of a man's life. Because it is requested and required of us so often in the Bible, I realized that this discipline must provide freedom. The mind is where most spiritual battles are won or lost. Your actions follow what you have already decided in your mind.

Step Eight, enjoying life with your wife, begins in your mind. Part of being disciplined in your mind means that you choose to think on the good. Give it some thought. Why do you keep reliving those bad moments of anger and resentment? Why aren't the good times replayed when you're in conflict with your wife or children? Remember that our enemy is smart. He wants us to feed on a diet of disease, not good food. Start by changing your diet and watch God work wonders in you.

Years ago, a professor performed a study with two different classes. The first class watched a movie that was filled with violence and revenge. The second class viewed a movie that was inspiring and redemptive. After each movie, he observed the students' interactions as he questioned each class. As you can imagine, the first class was less patient and more argumentative. Their comments were expressed with words of hopelessness. The second class demonstrated just the opposite. They were kinder to each other and their thoughts were more positive and hopeful.

One day, I had a particular thought come into my mind that robbed me of the good things God had given me. After much prayer, the Lord gave me this analogy. Do you remember 33-1/3 records? I think that the last one was produced in the early nineties. Remember when the needle would get caught in a groove and continue to replay the same words? I realized that I had made a groove in my thinking pattern and particular stimuli could hit my eyes and the needle would go right to that groove. This analogy taught me that I needed to pick up the arm that held the needle and move it. I did that in my mind each time the needle was stuck in that spot. It took some time, but soon the groove was smoother. God removed the groove, and the needle would just flow through and not skip.

In a Focus on the Family article called *Choose Your Rut Carefully* by Phil Callaway, he writes, "If we notice that the neighbor's grass is greener, let's remind ourselves that their water bill is probably higher, and they have to mow their lawn more often." Even looking at that other green grass steals your joy. I'm sure that this is why God firmly told us not to commit adultery or covet someone else's wife or possessions. Is it possible to refrain from doing this? I believe it is. Some like to say that this is just the way we men are, but I don't accept that. I don't say this lightly, because I do have some experience in this area.

If your head is always turning and mind lusting (mildly or strongly), I have found that this has very little to do with actually attractive women. It has more to do with your brokenness and an attempt to meet your needs in an unhealthy way. Let me give you an example. If you were dying of thirst in a desert with your mouth taped mouth shut, and someone poured cold water all over you, what would be the result? Eventually, you would still die of dehydration. No matter how much water was poured over your body, none would get inside where you needed it. In the same manner, looking, lusting, or committing adultery will not end your deepest desire for wholeness and personal fulfillment. As a matter of fact, this is exactly what Solomon discovered after all his indulgences — sexual and material: it was all in vain. He was still empty, even with the best the world had to offer him.

How do you become full, satisfied, and overjoyed with what you have and the woman that God gave you as a mate? In Andrew Jackson's farewell speech he said, "But you must remember, my fellow-citizens, that eternal vigilance by the people is the price of liberty, and that you must pay the price if you wish to secure the blessing." If you want to secure the blessings in your marriage, it will take the same dedication and vigilance. I believe that it takes vigilance to keep any of the good things God has given us in our lives — our faith, family, home, ministry, or job. Webster's Dictionary defines the state of being vigilant as being "alertly watchful especially to avoid danger." Being this alert might be hard at first, but it's the same as starting any good habit. When I first started to exercise on a regular basis, it took some effort. Soon it became something to look forward to, especially when I started to see some of the benefits. I feel stronger, have more endurance, I'm more alert, and I even look better. The outcome is only a result of the effort. It takes vigilance to do *The Ten* for your relationship with your wife and to be disciplined about the thoughts on which you meditate. Eventually the good results will come and these wholesome thoughts that honor God will produce an attitude of thankfulness and joy.

At a recent men's study I lead, we finished a great book I would recommend to you, *The Heart of a Tender Warrior* by Stu Weber. It's full of great advice and real life experiences. When we finished this book, we still had a few more weeks before we stopped for the summer. I prayed and asked the Lord to show me a good topic for the remaining weeks. The phrase "best practices" came into my mind. The first time I heard this phrase was in a customer's office. They told me that if I discovered a business practice that was really beneficial, I should share it with them so they could put it into practice in their business.

At our next meeting, I explained the definition of "best practices" and I asked the men to share their best practices regarding building relationships, handling arguments, fighting spiritual attacks, raising children, dating, and many others. We had fun telling others about our experiences and a great amount of wisdom was shared.

In chapter four, I talk about being a student of your wife. When I get excited about a subject, I find myself doing research, taking notes, and asking many questions of others. Recently, we are looking to downsize our home and find something on a lake that would offer more recreational activity for our grown kids and their children when they visit us. I did research, took notes, checked things out, and learned as much as I could. In a way, I became a student of real estate in our area. In the same way, I would suggest that you purchase a small notebook and use it to make observations of what your wife enjoys and what you enjoy doing together. One of the men in our group mentioned that his best practice was to notice the things that excited his wife, then secretly make plans to do this activity to surprise her. This works very well for day trips that you take the time to plan. It would also work for something as simple as choosing a place to eat.

TEN

Notice if she makes a comment about a restaurant she'd like to try as you drive by one, then let a little time pass before you take her. It's all about being tuned in to her desires and wishes, then doing your part in making these happen.

The follow through is what makes this best practice work. Some men are simply unwilling to take the time to do something nice for their wives. What do you think this communicates to her?

One of my friends at the gym is a man I'll call Tom, and he will be married thirty years this year. He knows where his wife really wants to go on a trip. He has plenty of airline miles to use and enough hotel points to get the entire vacation for free. We're talking about a weekend trip that is totally paid for. On several occasions, I've asked him how his planning was going. I'm fascinated with the list of things at work that he has placed ahead of this important event. I've given him many encouraging words to plan ahead so that the airline and hotel frequent users programs won't block out dates that he may want. I can see the train wreck coming with procrastination at the wheel. When I ask him what prevents him from putting this anniversary gift at the top of his priority list, the answer is always framed with, "I'm too busy." I continue to gently encourage him, but I'm afraid that the situation will not end well.

Please don't fall into this trap. Being a student of your wife is a choice that is based on your decision to love her. Make the choice to put her at the top of your priority list, not at the middle or bottom.

Your priorities will shift when you refocus your vision toward your wife to see her as a gift that God selected just for you. He will mold and shape you into the husband you are meant to be. It's a great place to be and at the same time you will see your wife blossom into the woman He created her to be.

11103

Many years ago I remember my dad telling me, "John, if you treat your wife right, she will open up and blossom like a rose." That made sense to me at the time. If you take a rose whose petals are closed and place it in water, the petals open and the rose looks beautiful. However, I didn't have the tools or the know-how to treat Rita the way she deserves to be treated. Now with the tool of *The Ten*, you know the steps to take to help you grow and become the man your wife and family need.

If you're having a hard time coming up with things to plan for your wife, casually ask her if she can recall some times with you that were special and what made them memorable. Take a walk down memory lane and focus only on the good times. You in turn can share some times that were special for you. Looking back, listening, and probing should give you many ideas of what to do for her in the future. If she asks why you're asking so many questions, there's no problem with telling her that you want to do a better job of knowing her — really knowing her.

One of the best ways you can enjoy your wife is to enjoy the things she loves. Most women love their children. Immediately after birth, I've seen many young women totally transformed. A mom's world completely changes her. What seemed like a life about fulfilling goals for themselves now modifies because of this little baby. We know of countless stories of ways that women have sacrificed everything for their children, some even give up their lives. When a man makes a conscious decision to value his children by taking time to teach, train, work, and play with them, it sends a huge message to your wife. Women love men who love the people and things that they love. Men, love the children that God and your wife have given you and this will establish a foundation of joy built on commitment and trust.

A few years ago, our middle son's wife, Carrie, gave birth to our first grandson, Elias. I'm sure that when our first son was born, Rita gave Jared just as much attention and love, but I didn't see it back then. I was so busy doing things that I missed seeing her face light up every time she looked at him. I missed seeing her bond with our first son, but now it's different. Because of God's wonderful grace, I am in the "now." I can take the time to observe my wife with our first grandchild. I see a woman who becomes so focused on this little guy that she lights up inside. I observe her every facial gesture, her funny sounds, and the way she gets his attention with her kind and loving words. I see that her greatest priority is to be part of his life and our kids' lives. I think that the most fulfilling thing for a woman is to know that her children and her children's children have become loving and nurturing men and women. This is what life is all about. Your job as a husband and father is to create an environment of commitment, safety, and respect that allows your loved ones to flourish.

Let's review. First, become a student of your wife by watching and learning about what she likes and dislikes. Make notes and be as observant as possible. Be very intentional about this. Review your findings with a fellow brother to brainstorm for other similar ideas. Next, take the time to do the planning. Remember that every plan does not need to be expensive. Most of the memorable things that Rita and I have done were not expensive, just thoughtful. You will find that when you do plan things that cost more money, they will continue to communicate the message of value to your wife.

Maybe it will never be like the Garden of Eden when things were perfect and easy, but with vigilance and a commitment to make the right choices, you can make a difference in your marriage. Meditate on the right things and continually ask God for His help and strength. You can do anything through faith.

Study Questions:
Chapter 8 — Enjoy your Life Together

1. When you lived at home, can you remember what your dad and mom enjoyed doing together? If your parents were separated, can you remember what other family members did for joy?

2. What are the first things you can remember worrying about? Can you think about what threatened you so much? Deep down can you determine what you were afraid of?

3. What continual negative or dishonoring thoughts go through your head? Have you acknowledged them? What steps can you take to restore your thought life?

4. What strategy do you think Satan has used on you? Do you have a weakness that he concentrates on? Try to write it out and share.

5. Share "best practices" in your group of what really works in each area.
   a.) Spiritual warfare
   b.) Studying your wife
   c.) Dates or occasions she loved

6. Start making observations or ask your wife what she would really enjoy. Share it in your group with your plan on how to accomplish it. Be open to other men's suggestions. Remember that there is wisdom in a multitude of counsel.

Chapter 9 — Don't Criticize Her: Appreciate Her
(Days 9, 19, 29)

A critical spirit or negative attitude can be your greatest tormentor and the most damaging thing to those around you. Over the years I've heard many excuses and rationalizations to justify this behavior. The ones I hear the most are, "That's just the way I am." "I can't help being honest. I call it the way I see it." "If I don't tell him, who will?" When several people are together and the person they're speaking about is not present, it's revealing how critical we can be. I must confess that I've been part of that group and I can be very tactful at putting in my hits. It takes a special effort for me to stop and listen to what I'm saying, because it is difficult for me to put on the brakes when I'm speaking.

Being critical, gossiping, or having a negative attitude can start innocently. It is usually a bad habit that you learned from someone else. But have you ever wondered how a bad habit can change from a simple habit to a heavy burden? Over the years I have formulated a theory regarding behavior based on my observations and personal experience. Now that I'm in my sixties, I've had a number of years to see if there is any validity to my theory and I can say it has proved itself. My theory is that if bad habits or character flaws are not addressed early, they become worse as time goes on.

There is hope for all of us, because as John Bradford said, "There but the grace of God go I." Many times I'm confronted with this destructive behavior in myself and I thank God that I have received His grace and I am making progress on addressing this issue and always growing in grace.

A critical spirit destroys and it is right out of the pit of hell. The very first "Mr. Negativity" was Satan himself, because he personifies negativity and criticalness. His first attack was aimed at Eve in the Garden of Eden when he attacked God's character. Satan has always been very clever and would never actually say, "God's not honest with you or Adam and you can't trust him. He holds back the good stuff, so you should take matters into your own hands." No. He wasn't this obvious, but that's what he was really saying when he told Eve, " 'You will not surely die,' the serpent said to the woman. 'For God knows that when you eat of it your eyes will be opened, and you will be like God, knowing good and evil.'" (Genesis 3:4-5) This was nothing similar to what God had told her.

Satan's strategy with Eve is the same one he uses on us today. First and most importantly, we must understand his character because his tactics are based on his nature and this nature is evil. There is no love within him, so he can't understand forgiveness, love, loyalty, and most of all he can't understand God's ways. Just being around him and listening to him make light of the things of God — from His creation to the character of God's people — would be a painful experience.

The real message Satan was trying to communicate to Eve was that God's character was not to be trusted. Always remember that when Satan says something about God, he reveals more about himself than about God. Satan was actually projecting his own critical nature. Satan only gives and projects what is in him — anger, resentment, envy, greed, bitterness, lust, hate, rage, and murder — and he has no insight or depth into things of real substance. When we respond to his actions with the love of God, it throws him every time. The Scriptures are very clear that our thoughts, words, and actions should be pleasing in God's sight.

Where do you think most of your negative and critical thoughts come from? Satan is totally captured by a critical spirit and that's where he wants to hold you as well. Can you imagine an existence of always looking for the bad and pointing out every defect you see? Remember that Paul calls him the "accuser of our brothers." (Revelation 12:10) "Mr. Negative" loves to go before our Lord and point out all of our shortcomings to God.

I do think that when Jesus told those who doubted him, "You belong to your father, the devil, and you want to carry out your father's desire. He was a murderer from the beginning, not holding to the truth, for there is no truth in him." (John 8:44), Jesus was saying that on many surfaces, their propensity was always to see the wrong side. They were masters at calling evil things good, and good things evil. Where do you think their ideas originated? There is only one source for this confusion, Satan.

How could they be this blind to the truth? The Pharisees are a great example of this because they spent so much of their lives pointing out sin and judging others that they couldn't receive the most wonderful miracles Jesus performed without looking for His faults.

Jesus was talking to his disciples when he said, "Be merciful, just as your Father is merciful. Do not judge, and you will not be judged. Do not condemn, and you will not be condemned. Forgive, and you will be forgiven. Give, and it will be given to you. A good measure, pressed down, shaken together and running over, will be poured into your lap. For with the measure you use, it will be measured to you." (Luke 6:36-38) What did He know about human nature that we do not? He knew that it was much easier for us to judge someone else's flaws than to do the hard work of changing ourselves. Church work can be very seductive in this way because Satan loves to see you running around trying to fix others because he knows you can't. Satan loves it when you live your life with the beam in your eye. At that point, you are still blind to the ways he can push your buttons.

Satan's manipulations aren't the only reason you might have a critical spirit (though he probably has a hand in these other ways also). Sometimes there is a deep hurt or pain that has not been resolved and your built up resentment about this is causing you to act out and hurt others. Don't be discouraged, we aim for progress, not perfection. The most important thing is a commitment to stay with it. There was a saying that I mentioned earlier in the book, "Hurt people, hurt people." If your hurts are left unhealed, you will hurt others. The most common way to hurt someone in this situation is with your tongue. Remember, if you're harboring resentment, you should consider the role you play in your healing or forgiving process as well.

There are many ways to avoid inner healing. Some may not look obvious to you, so let me ask you a few questions. Are you busy all the time — always at work, play, or even at church doing God's work — so that you're just running constantly? Over the years, I've known many committed Christians who were workaholics at their church. It was a great way to avoid dealing with personal issues. This isn't how He wants you to live and He wants you to face these hurts directly. It may not seem like it at the time, but when our Lord pulls the rug out from under you, it's a great gift. He is far more interested in you becoming real — an authentic person — so that you're not afraid of Him or yourself.

Another possible reason for a critical spirit is to help you feel better about yourself. Sometimes people put someone down to elevate themselves. When you do this, you are really saying, "Look how stupid that person is and how smart I am."

I heard a story about a man whose wife was a woman of faith before she got married. Over the years, she would share her faith with her husband and he would ridicule and mock it. When she was older, she became very ill and was not handling it well. Her husband asked her, "Why don't you call on your faith to comfort you now?" She responded, "I can't. You did too good a job destroying it."

Most of us could agree that we don't want to be the kind of husband who steals good qualities from our wives by being critical. Now that you are aware of the potential of a negative spirit, I want to tell you that this method is not acceptable and it won't work any longer. Whatever your motive is, being critical is like an acid: it eats away at yourself and others. If it is left unchecked, it will destroy you.

For many of us, our emotional growth was stunted early in life. There could have been some trauma that acted as the catalyst, but it happens without one too. When we stopped growing emotionally, we found other unhealthy ways to cope with pain and disappointment. Later in life, we realize that our old coping methods don't work anymore and we are faced with a decision to let go of our past and move forward. Being critical to cover up an old wound is a way to cope and we must let go of it. Are you ready to let go of your old destructive ways and reach out for healing?

Can this negative cycle be broken even if it has been going on for generations? Can you change even if you grew up in a critical and judgmental home? My answer is categorically, "Yes!" All things are possible with God. If you have given your life to Jesus Christ, you have the Holy Spirit living in you to empower you to live a transformed life. Earlier in the book I said, "Simple does not mean easy." Many of God's principles are simple, but they are not easy.

The following are some simple steps I've used that have helped me get away from my negative or critical spirit.

First you must recognize that this is a part of you. Any addict — alcoholic, drug user, or gambler — must first accept his bondage. Denial is the major block to any spiritual growth. If you are not sure this is an issue for you, ask family members or trusted friends. I am sure they will let you know if you are critical of them. Ask yourself if you a faultfinder. Be honest. Do you usually look for the good in a situation or the fault?

Let me pause for a minute. Even if you're not a big violator of this, consider that we all have our targets. Don't excuse yourself if you are critical of only one person. You can convince yourself that because it's only, "fill in the name," you don't have a problem. Look deeper into this before moving on and brushing it off because you might find a critical spirit at the root.

Once you accept that you are negative and critical, ask God to help you change. Know that it usually takes an overdose of any flaw before you see it in yourself. You didn't wake up one morning and decide to be critical, so it happened gradually and you've gotten used to it. At this point, it probably feels good to put down others so that you come across as the righteous one. This may be difficult for you to refrain from because you may miss the feeling of empowerment or of elevating yourself above others.

The key is to let God work on you and not to think that this is a solo job. I've never known a person to be healed emotionally by his own strength or desire. We must admit to God, ourselves, and another human being the exact nature of our wrongs. Don't be deceived, it's only pride that prevents you from doing this and this false pride keeps you in captivity.

After you have accepted your flaw, pray for an accountability partner to work with you on this shortcoming. Let him know what you are trying to do and that you need him to be there for you and pray for you. The apostle James said, "Therefore confess your sins to each other and pray for each other so that you may be healed. The prayer of a righteous man is powerful and effective." (James 5:16)

Once you have a brother who has agreed to help you get rid of this critical habit, do a very focused inventory. Find a quiet place and ask the Lord to bring to mind the times you were critical and negative. Write down each situation to the best of your ability. Be completely thorough and honest with yourself in this process.

When you have done this, ask the Lord to show you why you responded that way. Then go over your responses with your partner. I'm sure the Lord will bring to mind the root of this behavior if it still persists. Seek out people in your church who are committed to prayer. Ask them to pray for you and if possible to even pray over you.

Jesus offers us hope, faith, transformation, and forgiveness. One of the most meaningful moments in Mel Gibson's *The Passion of the Christ* was to see Jesus carry the cross and stumble. He looked at his mother and said, "I've come to make all things new." Yes, He has come to make all things new — even us. We just have to be willing. It is crucial for us to allow Him to change us and it's vital for us to comply with His guidance. Men, we must learn to be teachable and always put aside pride and ego.

Many of us will continually ask God to change us. Faith comes in when we move forward and act on what we asked. To become a new creature, you first need to act like one. I am convinced that Jesus can heal instantly. However, it has been my experience in emotional healing that He takes you through a much longer process. My personal view is that He wants you to experience the time it takes to grow in emotional maturity. Growing is not rooted in quick fixes, but in patience.

If you feel that you remain stuck, continue to ask God for help. I know it's hard because you might have a closet full of things you have said and done that hurt those around you. Just remember that our enemy, Satan, wants to keep you in bondage with shame and guilt, but God wants you set free. He will provide the right men in your life to help.

Now you are aware that you need to stop looking for the negative. The big questions remains: how do you learn to appreciate someone? It's pretty simple: just look for the good. Each time you want to be negative, stop yourself. You should rebuke it in Jesus' name and replace it with a reminder to look for the good.

I became so much more appreciative of Rita when I started to see all of the good traits she has. This might sound simplistic, but women have some very important attributes that men lack. One I've recently noticed in Rita is her intuitiveness. She has a much greater awareness of people's intents, whether they are positive or negative. She (and I think many women) can spot a phony much more quickly than a man. Women can also read danger signs better. Men, I think when we try to project manliness, we can behave like we really know what's going on, when in fact we might be deceived. I really value Rita's opinions in this area and this is one way to show my appreciation of her.

Looking for the good really means to value your differences. One difference of ours that always comes to my mind is my wife's ability to make our house a home. She is extremely gifted in decorating, knowing the right colors, fabrics, furniture, and everything to do with the interior of our home. I have to confess that I am oblivious to all of these things. I was even a hindrance for a long time to the changes she wanted to make in our home. I was so focused on not spending any money that I would just try to make do with what we had. Eventually we came up with a plan to renovate in small steps that we both felt comfortable with.

One morning, Rita asked me to look across the room to see if I noticed anything different. I didn't see anything until she pointed out some new curtains. If it were up to me, our home would be a mess. But because she was persistent with the changes and her great gift in design, I love coming home — it's warm, comfortable, and inviting — it is a very special place. When our children or friends come to visit, it is so inviting that they feel like they're in a bed-and-breakfast.

I see now that I was penny wise and pound-foolish about these renovations she wanted to make. Because of all the good choices she made, our home is now worth much more. I had such a blind spot.

Another area that I appreciate about Rita is her generous spirit. Over the years, time and time again, she has put our children above her own wants and needs. When our middle son, Adam, went off to college, he met many young men from different kinds of homes. Years later when we were celebrating Rita's fiftieth birthday, he mentioned that he thought that all mothers made breakfast for their children. However, when he was at school, his friends told him just how special that was. Rita is special to all of us. She loves spending time with her sons and sitting around the breakfast table was one way she found to spend time with them. She made them a priority and I know that they value that. By observing her over the years, it has become apparent how important our family is to her.

Rita also brings a positive difference to our family in her ability to create memorable vacations for our family. When I was growing up, we didn't have family vacations. I only remember my father taking us somewhere once. Rita grew up in a home where her family would go to a lake house or beach often. To this day, she has great memories of her dad in this setting, cooking and having lots of fun. Her Uncle Pete had a great cabin that was near a lake and ski lodge and this was a wonderful place for their family to go. I really enjoyed these trips with her family when I was dating her.

Needless to say, our family carried on Rita's family's great tradition. Between my parents' home on the ocean in Florida to summer rentals on the Outer Banks, we have had more than twenty years of wonderful family vacations, laughs, games, and memories. She was the one who always made sure we found the money to do it because she wanted to invest both her time and money in family time. Now that our children are adults, we all care very deeply for each other. We have all of these wonderful shared memories.

I don't have to look very far to see the good that Rita has imparted to all of us. I would suggest doing the same with your wife and family. Look for the good your wife brings to your relationship. Then thank God for her.

Study Questions:
Chapter 9 — Don't Criticize Her: Appreciate Her

1. When you are critical, where do you think it comes from? Does it help or hurt you and those around you?

2. Who was the most critical person of you when you were growing up? Who always looked for the good in you?

3. Have you ever said, "This is just the way I am. I can't change." Do you think the God of all creation who made you, the stars, and planets can't help you?

4. Have you ever considered that Satan can't comprehend love or forgiveness? Have you ever struggled with forgiveness? Why?

5. When you look for the good in your wife, list what you see.

6. What are some ways you can start appreciating your wife?

Chapter 10 — Do Things for Her That Mean Something to Her (Days 10, 20, 30)

This step is another difficult one because it requires placing your wife (and family) before yourself. As I write this chapter, many memories of my selfish acts in the last forty-one years of marriage stream through my head. Scripture tells us that "[Jesus] humbled himself and became obedient to death — even death on a cross!" (Philippians 2:8) Every step in this book starts with Jesus. The Apostle Paul reminds us, "Each of you should look not only to your own interests, but also to the interests of others. Your attitude should be the same as that of Christ Jesus: Who, being in very nature God, did not consider equality with God something to be grasped, but made himself nothing, taking the very nature of a servant, being made in human likeness." (Philippians 2:4-7)

An example of Jesus in the form of a servant can be found in the story about the last night Jesus spent with His disciples, traditionally known as the Last Supper. After they ate, Jesus took a basin of water and towel, then he proceeded to wash the feet of the disciples. This act of service, along with many others in scripture, has taken on a deeper meaning for me as I get older.

I am now in my sixties and I still can't understand how the creator of all things humbled Himself to wash dirty, dusty feet as an example to us. With His words, "Now that I, your

Lord and Teacher, have washed your feet, you also should wash one another's feet. I have set you an example that you should do as I have done for you." (John 13:14-15) It seems like we have an example of Jesus' selflessness in every situation in which we might want to act selfishly. In spite of being wrongfully accused and abused, He responded with unprecedented love. From serving others to forgiving the ones who nailed Him to the cross, He leaves no room for our excuses; we must do the same.

The more I read scripture I find myself confronted with the words of the missionary Jim Elliot, "He is no fool who gives up what he cannot keep to gain that which he cannot lose." The giving up of one's self is simple, but certainly not easy. Even still, it is more difficult to give up our own desires to take on the form of a servant to those around us. Our own brokenness and natural needs cry out at times. What needs do you have that keep you from giving up your desires completely? How can you possibly serve your wife and family when you still hunger for your own needs to be met? That's a very good question, and it's easy to find ourselves in this perplexing state.

I have to admit that I've been one who yearns for my needs to be met by those around me. My neediness has a great potential to get in the way of God's growth and development in me. Usually I look to Rita to meet my needs first. Looking back, I can see that the burden I used to give solely to her was a heavy one. I can recall the pressure I placed on her — sometimes subtle, but at other times more obvious — for affirmation, sex, and a host of other need-driven desires. Please let me reiterate that I know we were created to have healthy desires. I'm not saying that we have to squash those. What I am expressing is that we might be trying to fix our problems in the wrong way. There is a saying that I've often used, "The quicker the fix is, the worse the solution." Needs met immediately are quick fixes and they will lead to bad outcomes.

A very good example of a quick fix/bad outcome can be seen in the pornography industry. Pornography fills one's mind with all kinds of images offering some kind of satisfaction to our brokenness. What's the outcome? We become even thirstier for the wrong cure and we spiral down until God has mercy on us when we cry out for help.

Satan actually puts thoughts in our minds to elevate our neediness. His own neediness drives him, although his needs will never be met. He is destined to eternal suffering because he constantly rejects the true source of peace. His goal is to deceive you into thinking that there are other ways to find your wholeness. The only way to fill the void of these needs and desires is with the acceptance and gift of grace from Jesus Christ.

There isn't one story about Jesus in the Bible where He turned a situation around to make it about His needs. Even as I write these words, I am amazed. "For even the Son of Man did not come to be served, but to serve, and to give his life as a ransom for many." (Mark 10:45) He was nailed — yes, nailed — to a hard wooden cross to purchase our freedom. For each of us, there was a time when we were not free. We were all under the devil's influence at some time, captive to his destructive plans, trapped in an ongoing struggle, and without the power to free ourselves from the deception of his illusions. The moment we opened our hearts to the Lord and asked Him into our lives, we were set free.

I used to think that men just needed to know the truth and see the picture with clarity, then they would get down to the hard work of making God a part of their restoration. I have found that as important as this is, it's not the reason they don't change. Men, our denial and self-centeredness run so deep that I'm afraid it sabotages what God wants to do in us. Remember that ego stands for "easing God out."

Perseverance is one of the greatest character strengths God has put in us, but it can also be our greatest weakness when we won't let go of something. Our own selfish stubbornness is our worst enemy. As Pogo said, "We have met the enemy and he is us." This is such a dilemma for men. It is so much easier to yield to our desires rather than work for the things God desires for us. Pray and ask God to help you let go of the needs and desires you are still holding on to. Remember that He is the only one who can bring you fulfillment.

In the Old Testament, there is a story of a commander of an army who develops leprosy. His wife's servant, a young girl, tells him about a prophet named Elisha and convinces the commander to see him. When the commander visits Elisha, the prophet tells him to bathe in the Jordan River seven times. At this advice, the commander became angry and said that it was beneath him to do such a stupid thing. The commander's servants said, "My father, if the prophet had told you to do some great thing, would you not have done it? How much more, then, when he tells you, 'Wash and be cleansed!' So he went down and dipped himself in the Jordan seven times, as the man of God had told him, and his flesh was restored and became clean like that of a young boy." (2 Kings 5:13-14) The bottom line was that his pride prevented him from going into the river. Once the commander renounced his false pride, he did as the prophet told him and became totally healed.

Have you faced your own false pride about doing what your wife wants? If you are like most of us, you are probably still clinging to it. My question for those of you who are struggling to let go of your pride and ego is: has your way worked? If not, stop fighting this new way. Accept a new way of living and just do it.

Jesus reminds us that we contend against the devil, the world, and our own sinful nature. Each of these obstacles has their own set of challenges that we continually face. The world and its messages scream out at us, "You deserve the best of everything. Go for it." Many men still believe that the world has the answer in materialism, success, or pleasure. Others realize that we should wear the world like a light coat that is easy to take off.

We have a saying in my men's group: "You get help when you become sick and tired of being sick and tired." Unfortunately, I've seen a large majority of men get to such a painful place that they just can't go on. They need to get rid of the pain, either by dealing with it in an emotionally unhealthy way (like drowning their pain in alcohol or covering it up with work) or resorting to a more physical method of dealing with pain. I'm always amazed at how much pain a man can endure before he surrenders to God's plan for him.

Over the years, I have worked with men in many different settings and there comes a time for each of us when we get stuck. Some men leave the group so that they aren't confronted with their issue and some men prefer to remain stuck. I have no idea why some men drop out of the process to wholeness. After fourteen years of doing twelve-step work, I have heard many excuses from men as to why they refuse to work on their character flaws. It is very common for men to be blind to their flaws and refuse to take responsibility for them. Allow me to encourage you to press on — don't give up or even just stay where you are. With *The Ten*, you now have a tool that will help you when you feel stagnant. Please choose to face your pain in the best possible way. Choose to face it head on.

A temptation when dealing with tough issues is to point your finger to blame someone else. The easiest targets are your wife, parents, boss, or children. Did you ever notice that when you point your finger at someone there are always three fingers pointing back? From the very beginning in the garden with Adam and Eve, the finger pointing started. She blamed the serpent and Adam blamed his wife. A similar blame game goes on today. We usually like to blame others for how we behave, even though this eventually runs out. When you run out of options of people to blame, you may be forced to take responsibility for your own actions. Then you will see that you have actually allowed another person to have control over you. Then you must choose to take responsibility for your choices. With God's help, He will help you to regain control of your life and learn to react to situations without blaming someone else.

To completely deal with your needs and desires, we need to dig deep into why they are there. Anybody who does any gardening knows that just pulling off the tops of weeds does not really remove them. You need to get the entire root out, hence the old adage, "Get to the root of the problem." Many of us have had generational cycles of the same problem because the root cause has never been dealt with. Someone has to stop passing it on and because you're engaging in *The Ten*, I think that someone is you. Unless you deal with the root of these issues, the cycle will continue to your children and your children's children. If you need some evidence of this, look around at the men who keep falling for the same bait. Many men continue to stay in debt, are involved in superficial relationships that lack depth, or struggle with use of pornography.

A cycle that is one of the easiest to slip into, but is the most damaging to those around you is to say and communicate hurtful words to your loved ones. By a husband's actions, some even communicate to their wives and children that they believe the members of their family are incapable of doing anything right. I know you don't wake up each morning saying, "How can I undermine my wife and kids' self esteem." It just happens. Remember, the Bible speaks a lot about our tongue. We choose to speak words that can bless or words that can kill.

With the experience of over nineteen years of work in a father-son program and thirty-seven years of parenting, I find that modeling is the most powerful way we communicate to our children. If you want your children to love their mother and ultimately to love their mate, you must be a model for them. Letting go of your own needs and making the choice to do meaningful things for your wife not only shows her that you love and value her, but your children will be better off for seeing it. Your loving actions and caring words are a cornerstone to harmony in your home. Whatever it takes, don't bolt when this seems difficult or even impossible.

When you're really ready to make some serious changes, take your wife on your next date and ask her what you could do to communicate to her that she is "the one." Then listen carefully. Ask her for suggestions for you to work on. Ask her to be patient with you and let her know that you will be putting in the hard work to make these changes.

Meet with each of your children privately and let them know the ways that you want to change. Ask them to describe some ways you have offended them. In situations where you could change, make the changes and start amending your behavior. If you do these two things, you're off to the right start.

Have you ever fished? Imagine going to just any lake, picking out just any hook, using any bait, and trying to catch a fish. Real fishermen leave nothing to chance. They know a lot about the places they fish — the best time of day to fish, the best water temperature, the ways weather is a factor, the best rod and hooks to use, and the most tempting bait to select — it all plays a part in the success of catching a fish. The best fishermen carefully study and research all of these things. I believe that most of us use the wrong rod, hook, and bait in attracting our wives' attention and communicating that we love her. Your wife needs certain things from you to feel loved and to blossom.

It is possible to study your wife in this same way. First you must really want to. Ask the Lord to give you the desire and insight to study your wife. Then follow through to give her what she needs. In Gary Chapman's book, *The Five Love Languages*, he explains that we each need to be shown love in different ways. When we try to show our wife we care, we can use a variety of approaches — affirming words, touch, gifts, quality time, and acts of service. Usually, one or two ways would be more meaningful to your wife than the others. These are referred to as her love language.

I remember when it became obvious to me that Rita's love language was acts of service. If I'm totally honest with you, I must admit that I mostly enjoy doing only what I want to do, not what Rita wants me to do. I really had to make an extra effort to change. Until recently, we lived in an old farmhouse on three acres of land in Connecticut. I thoroughly enjoyed taking care of the grounds and outside of the house. That kind of work is not work for me because I truly enjoy it. However, I don't like doing dishes, the floors, shopping, or painting inside. From this book, I learned that when I do those particular things for Rita, they are an act of service that she appreciates and communicates to her that I love her. Unfortunately I have to force myself to do these things, especially to clean out the cats' litter box. This is not brain surgery and you might even think it's foolish, but it's true that doing these acts for Rita are very meaningful to her and communicate my love for her. We share her second love language, which is quality time, so this one is easier for me. I just have to remind myself to keep the focus on her by asking her to express her thoughts.

Look for a variety of ways to fill your wife's emotional love tank. Just remember that it might take a while to see some changes, but you must be persistent each and every day. It has to be an intentional decision to keep her tank full. It's been said that if you can do something new for ninety days, it will become a habit.

In six months, you should ask each member of your family how you're doing. And then listen! Don't become defensive or excuse yourself. Accept what you hear, then talk it over with your partner on this journey. You will then have proof that this method works.

Lastly, I want to remind you that our enemy will use many tactics to derail you. You probably won't see any visible progress for a while, which will discourage you and cause you to want to give up. We have a saying in our men's group, "Don't stop until you see the miracle." God is always more interested in your character growth than your comfort. Put comfort on hold for a while — it won't kill you. Accept the growing process and just do what you know is the next right thing to do.

Also keep in mind that you're in this for the long haul. A large ship takes a long time to make a course correction after the rudder is turned. Keep the rudder in the new direction and the ship will turn. That's what will make the difference for the future of your family.

Study Questions:
Chapter 10 — Do Things for Her
That Mean Something to Her

1. What do you do that your wife would consider selfish?

2. There is power in words. What are some of the affirming words you are not speaking to your family?

3. What needs do you have that you would like to be met by your wife that she currently does not meet? Are they reasonable? Is there a deeper reason for these needs and why they continue? Discuss this with your wife.

4. What generational cycles run in your family that have hurt you and others? What do you think is the root of the problem?

5. Do you know your wife's love language? What were the clues?

6. List the things that you can do for her that really mean something to her.

Conclusion

Your wife has probably seen your very best moments and your very worst. Some of you might have just been married; others have been married a long time. Whether the length of your marriage is one year or thirty, there is a history that only the two of you share. There is something very special about that. Do all you can to nurture it.

Keep in mind that God has made us stewards of all the things He has given us. We should care for them and treat them as if they were on loan from Him. When it comes to your wife and family, consider your stewardship. Your family has been given to you on loan from God. Do your very best.

There are several things we can know about heaven and there are many things we won't know until we get there. One thing I can tell you with all certainty is that eternity is a long time. Even though at times, this life can be difficult, it is over in the blink of an eye in comparison. You won't be able to change your past, but with our Lord, you can change your future. Your tomorrows can be different.

Start making today count for eternity. I have every confidence in the fact that you can do that. My wife and children's destinies and who they are today all started with God. Surrender to His will for you. Do it today and don't stop.

Helpful tips and reminders

Discouragement can come in many shapes and sizes – from thoughts you can't stand in yourself to continual slips – but there are some ways you can combat these problems:

1. Seek prayer. Find a vibrant prayer group and ask for prayer as you work through *The Ten*.
2. Share your process with another brother. Make regular times to meet so you can encourage one another.
3. Fast. Jesus recommended it in scripture many times. There are many good resources on this subject.
4. Read Scripture each day. When you feel discouraged, recite Scripture as truth.
5. When circumstances look the bleakest, tell God exactly how you feel. Then trust Him and believe He understands the way you feel and thank Him for that.
6. Never give up. Our life on earth is short and you can never go wrong by doing what's right.

Dear Mrs. _____,

Your husband has agreed to take the most personally challenging program for married men. This course has the ability to transform your husband and your marriage and is just the beginning of a process of positive changes in your household. I originally designed this program for husbands as a simple word of mouth program. There was no way for a wife to find out the positive steps he was taking. That way, you would notice the good differences on your own.

However, at this point, you are probably aware of the men's study that your husband is involved with and you are accustomed to asking him about what they are studying in their group. There is also a book that accompanies this study, so it is not as simple as it once was. May I make a suggestion to you as your husband follows through with this program?

It would be my desire, as the developer of the program and author of the book your husband is reading, that you be more of an observer and receiver of what takes place, not an active participant. As strange as it may seem to you right now, trust that it is for the best if your husband does not give you details about the program. All your husband needs from you is encouragement as you see positive changes.

If you would like to be more actively involved, you may want to write your husband a letter that includes some ways you would like to see your relationship improve. Mention some things you would like to see him do better. Seal the letter in an envelope and put it in a safe place where you can find it later. This letter is not for him to read, but for you to keep track of the ways he improves. Keep a journal about things that surprise you or that seem out of the ordinary. In six months, look back to your original letter and see if anything is different.

I want you to know that it is my passion for a husband to become the man God wants him to be for his wife and family. The step your husband is now taking has the potential of changing marriages in your family for the better forever.

In advance, please let me thank you for your understanding and support.

God Bless,
John DePasquale

Cut these out and place them somewhere you will see them everyday. The small one is the size of a business card, so it will fit in your wallet. The larger one might be good for your briefcase or calendar. Just remember to put it somewhere your wife will not find it!

Ten – Transforming Life Series Ten Steps:

1. Listen to Her
2. Value Her: She's a Priority
3. Spend Time with Her: She's a Priority
4. Acknowledge Her Worth: Say It
5. Laugh and Enjoy Her More
6. Accept Her as She Is: Don't Try to Change Her
7. Show Her Compassion
8. Enjoy Your Life Together
9. Don't Criticize Her: Appreciate Her
10. Do Things for Her that Mean Something to Her

Ten – Transforming Life Series Ten Steps:

1. Listen to Her
2. Value Her: She's a Priority
3. Spend Time with Her: She's a Priority
4. Acknowledge Her Worth: Say It
5. Laugh and Enjoy Her More
6. Accept Her as She Is: Don't Try to Change Her
7. Show Her Compassion
8. Enjoy Your Life Together
9. Don't Criticize Her: Appreciate Her
10. Do Things for Her that Mean Something to Her

Bibliography

BOOKS
1. *The Serenity Bible: A Companion for Twelve Step Recovery* (Nashville: Thomas Nelson, 1990).
2. Gary Chapman, *The Five Love Languages* (Chicago: Northfield Publishing, 1992).
3. Robert S. McGee, *The Search for Significance* (Nashville: Thomas Nelson, 1990).
4. Gary Smalley and John Trent, Phd, *The Blessing* (Nashville: Thomas Nelson, 1993).
5. Stu Weber, *The Heart of a Tender Warrior* (Colorado Springs: Multnomah Publishing Group, 1993)

VIDEOS
1. Gary Smalley, *Hidden Keys to Loving Relationships* (Relationships Today, 1994).

MOVIES
1. *Jerry McGuire* (TriStar Pictures, 1996).
2. *The Passion of the Christ* (Newmarket Films, Fox, 2004).
3. *Patton* (20th Century Fox, 1970).